Men in Knits

Men in Knits

*Sweaters to Knit that
He WILL
Wear*

Tara Jon Manning

 **INTERWEAVE PRESS**

Editor: Jennifer Worick
Technical editor: Lori Gayle
Photography: Joe Coca
Photo styling: Karen Schober, Leigh Radford
Cover and interior design: Karen Schober
Illustrations: Ann Swanson
Production: Samantha L. Thaler
Copy editor: Stephen Beal
Proofreader and indexer: Nancy Arndt

Interweave Press gratefully acknowledges the cooperation of the following organizations, businesses, and individuals: Downtown and University Hill Management Division/Parking Services of the City of Boulder, Boulder Creek Events Winter Skate, City of Boulder Open Space and Mountain Parks, Chautauqua Park and Dining Hall, Stage House II, Trident Café, University Bicycles, Triana's, Montgomery House, Spruce Confections, Fast Eddie's, Todd and Alex Lessman, Dr. Bob Baxt, Tracy Ehlers and Alma, Nancy Kornblum and Bessie, Fred Hess, Juanita's.

Text copyright © 2003 Tara Jon Manning
Illustrations copyright © 2003 Interweave Press, Inc.
Photography copyright © 2003 Joe Coca and Interweave Press, Inc.

 Interweave Press, Inc.
201 East Fourth Street
Loveland, Colorado 80537-5655
www.interweave.com

Printed in Singapore by Tien Wah Press

Library of Congress Cataloging-in-Publication Data

Manning, Tara Jon, 1968-
  Men in knits : sweaters he will wear / Tara Jon Manning.
    p. cm.
Includes bibliographical references and index.
  ISBN 1-931499-23-3
  1. Knitting—Patterns. 2. Sweaters. 3. Men's clothing. I. Title.
TT825.M18 2003
746.43'20432—dc21
                                    2003004091

10 9 8 7 6 5 4 3 2 1

With love to Bill and Jack Manning, my sweater guys

—TJM

Contents

ACKNOWLEDGMENTS

Thanks to . . .

. . . all my loved ones, but especially to my husband Bill and my son Jack for making my dreams come true, for being the loves of my life, for patiently trying on every single sweater and subjecting themselves to the itchy test of every single yarn.

. . . the many manufacturers and distributors who graciously supplied the materials for the projects in this book.

. . . the talented knitters who helped make sweaters out of ideas—Diane Carlson, Lynn Gates, Mireille Holland, Marilyn King, and Judy Pearce.

. . . Interweave Press for bringing this book into being and to Lori Gayle, Leigh Radford, Karen Schober, and Jennifer Worick for their superb talents in making it be.

. . . the memory of Mister Fred Rogers, the ultimate sweater guy.

. . . all the patient guys out there who love their knitters and know the magic of wearing beautiful handknitted sweaters!

Introduction

MAKING A SWEATER that a man will actually wear—more than once!—is a challenging undertaking, to say the least. Although they may not want to admit it, guys can be awfully picky about their clothes. *Men in Knits* is meant to provide you with all the tools for making the right choices in fit, color, fiber, and style. Once you're sure of these details, every sweater will be enjoyable for you to knit and a joy for the men in your life to wear.

This book is intended to inspire you to knit for all your favorite guys—husbands, sons, brothers, dads, and friends (and maybe yourself, too!). You will learn how to make the best style and color choices for any guy, and how to investigate the way he determines his preferences and what kind of clothes he sees himself wearing.

The *Men in Knits* design collection offers twenty classic, stylish, and versatile sweaters to choose from. With your guy's help, you can choose from the book's designs and customize any pattern to incorporate the right style, color, yarn, and fit so you can knit a sweater that he *will* wear.

Part One:

How to Make His Favorite Sweater

Chapter 1:

What, Exactly, Does a Guy Want in a Sweater?

To learn the truth about why guys do—or more importantly, *don't*—like to wear sweaters, I abandoned convoluted theories and instead returned to the basics. In other words, I asked them. I went straight to the source and conducted an informal anonymous survey, recruiting volunteers to fill out questionnaires at a local coffee shop or via e-mail. The guys who participated in this far-from-scientific experiment provided some valuable and predictable information about what they want in a sweater. The respondents were mainly career professionals from a variety of fields—managers, engineers, and students—with a chef, firefighter, and construction manager mixed in.

Most men surveyed answered that they prefer pullovers and use them for casual, off-the-job wear. Those who prefer pullovers opt for crewnecks and turtlenecks. They like these sweaters for the following factors: versatility, warmth, ease of wear, and roominess. Men who prefer V necks and cardigans are professionals and older guys who like the styles for comfort around the neck and their ability to dress up. One in four guys likes big, bulky sweaters that make him look and feel rugged and brawny.

Most men in the survey indicate that sweaters are part of both their casual and dressy wardrobe; a few say they wear sweaters only for special occasions. Most like sweaters that are versatile enough for both casual and dressy events. Their most popular reason for choosing a sweater is fit, followed by style, color, and comfort/warmth. And you thought they don't care much about that kind of stuff!

Most guys feel that color and fiber are important, and they look for warmth and softness. Many want a yarn that's easy to care for. Their favorite colors are dark, and include navy and other blues, green, black, and brown, although they *say* they don't know why they prefer these colors. Those who cited specific reasons say that certain colors make them feel good, complement their skin tone, or look good with their eyes.

All but one guy in the survey have knitters in their lives—hurray! Most men say that someone has made them a handknitted sweater; most say they like the sweater but rarely wear it. By and large, these guys have been involved in pattern, yarn, and color selection. Those who like their handknitted sweaters say they are well-made and warm. Those who do not like or wear their sweaters cite bad color and bad fit. So, if they participate in the yarn and style selection, what goes wrong?

Making It a Favorite

Consider that almost all the men I surveyed who were dissatisfied with their sweaters said that they did in fact participate in choosing the pattern and the yarn. For the most part, these guys liked the color but little else. The fit and the style of the sweater missed the mark.

The first step to ensuring a happy ending to your guy's sweater story is to involve him in *every* step of the process in a fun and effortless way. If you attempt to collect information when his focus is elsewhere or he is obviously not in the mood, back off and try again later. If you force the issue, you run the risk of turning him off from the process entirely.

> Do you want to make a sweater he will enjoy wearing, or do you want to knit a project you will enjoy?

In addition to keeping him involved, you need to think about whether you are making the sweater for him to wear or for you to knit. At first blush, this may not seem like a tricky question, but ponder it a moment. If he chooses the most boring stockinette stitch pullover style in the world, will you push him to pick again, suggesting something a little more interesting to knit? If his color choice is chocolate brown—which you find "ho-hum" and boring, not to mention just like the other three sweaters you have made him—will you steer him toward a brighter shade or a Kaffe Fasset-style intarsia piece? You need to ask yourself what your goal is. Do you want to make a sweater he will enjoy wearing, or do you want to

knit a project you will enjoy? First and foremost, you should be making something *he* likes, or everyone's time is wasted. Don't try to enhance his wardrobe with something you find interesting; give him something he wants to wear. The information and the projects in this book will enable you to make everyone happy. Save the patchwork intarsia for yourself or your home.

Contrary to popular opinion, men really do care about things; they just care differently than women do. Women tend to think that men are oblivious and not very picky. If you hold this view, do not ask for his input, and make him something anyway; you may be sadly surprised by just how finicky he turns out to be. If you want to create something that will see the light of day outside of a drawer or closet, carefully explain to him the kinds of decisions on which you need his input; otherwise he won't realize he has a problem until he's wearing it.

> The information and the projects in this book will enable you to make everyone happy. Save the patchwork intarsia for yourself or your home.

This book explains the major categories of contemporary men's style. It helps you learn how to educate both yourself and your guy about his personal style. After conducting a skin-tone evaluation to determine his best colors, you and he will decide together on the best fiber for his sweater. You will consider his existing wardrobe and favorite colors in the selection process. You will work through a list of what to measure and how to take exact measurements. Armed with this data, you will be able to categorize his body type, identify specific fit issues, and learn ways to customize his sweater.

As you explore this design collection, you will find suggestions on which sweaters suit which guys. Every sweater is designed with a bit of classic style to ensure that it's worn year after year. The patterns are accessible to beginning and intermediate knitters, yet they offer enough interest to engage the most seasoned expert.

> If he says he will not wear a sweater, he probably isn't kidding.

Choosing the right color, making it fit, making it personalized, and making it well will ensure that the sweater you knit will stand the test of time and be the one that he reaches for again and again.

Treading on Dangerous Ground

At one time or another, we have all firmly believed that we really could change someone, sway his opinion, or influence his point of view. This is dangerous ground to tread on, and it's been the basis of many a heartbreak and breakup. Sadly, I feel this is true about the issue of "sweater guy" versus "not-a-sweater guy." As a knitter, you want nothing more than to knit for those you hold dear, infusing each stitch with love and magic. However, if he says he will not wear a sweater, he probably isn't kidding.

If this is the case, do yourself, him, and your relationship a favor and do not make him a sweater. At least not yet. Start small. Ask him some of the suggested questions. If he's receptive, determine his personal style and best colors. Use

> Like women, men should also have the prerogative to change their minds once in a while.

this information to work your mojo into a scarf or another knitted accessory. If he has a change of heart based on the unparalleled softness and beauty of the finished piece, not to mention the unending compliments he receives while wearing it, perhaps you can "reluctantly" agree to make him that sweater he said he didn't want. Like women, men should also have the prerogative to change their minds once in a while.

The Dreaded Boyfriend Curse

"I made him a sweater and he broke up with me!" You've heard this one before, right? Has it ever stopped you from knitting something for a special guy? Why does the idea of a curse persist? Here are a few theories.

▪ The knitting of the sweater outlives the relationship. Sad but true, we've all seen it happen.

▪ The knitted garment, while perhaps made of lightweight yarn, indicates too heavy or serious a commitment. Squeamish guys may start sweating when you offer to make them a *sandwich*, so don't take it personally when they reject your sweater.

▪ Making him something smacks of Mom. If this is the case, cut him loose now: He doesn't appreciate your passion and craft.

▪ The sweater represents hours and hours focused on him, and that freaks him out. He starts to think you are more into him than he is into you.

▪ You're the giver and he's the taker, and he suddenly feels obligated to you. The power has shifted and he doesn't like it.

▪ He hates what you knit because of size, color, style, itch factor, or whatever, and figures that you don't understand him at all.

You probably have a few other theories to add to the list but rest assured, with the information and patterns in this book, you will never suffer the sting of the boyfriend curse again.

Chapter 2:

Defining His Personal Style

❧

The journey to his perfect sweater begins with research and dialogue. To formulate the ultimate sweater, you need to determine four basic components: his personal style, the right color, the right yarn, and the right fit.

Understanding His Personal Style

Using his personal style as the cornerstone to choosing the right sweater design is crucial, but first you need to define his style category. Personal style is largely fantasy and image-based; it is how he wants to be perceived by others, even by himself. While personal style is what a man wants his clothes to say about him, it also takes into account his age, wardrobe preferences, and actual and desired activities. According to the diversity of his lifestyle, a guy can fall into more than one category, but one style will dominate. For example, consider the young professional who spends his weekends at a cabin or on his mountain bike. If he is indeed a style schizophrenic, work with him to determine whether he wants a sweater suitable for multiple settings or geared toward one situation.

Personal style is broken down into three general categories based on current fashion trends, traditional styles of men's dress, and information coll-ected from survey participants. The categories are:

- ■ Young Men's/Active Casual
- ■ Young Professional/Modern Casual
- ■ Corporate/Traditional.

Young Men's/Active Casual

This category is perhaps the most media- and image-based of the three. It is also the category that most guys move through and probably return to at varying stages. Its fundamental spirit is the youthful, athletic, preppy look presented by menswear retailers such as Abercrombie & Fitch, J. Crew, and Polo. The typical guy in this category falls into a teenage to thirty-something age range. He wishes he had—or maybe still has—those totally cut abs shown in clothing ads. He tries very hard to capture that contradictory "I don't care" bedhead look that is also perfectly groomed and precisely put together. This guy rarely tucks in a shirt.

Outdoor enthusiasts also fall into this category, even if they are only weekend warriors. Fleece lovers, performance-gear guys, and recreationists of every sort embrace the rugged and outdoor essence of the Active Casual component of this category. They exude an easygoing, casual vibe, which they carry with them as they evolve or straddle two categories. The Young Men's/Active Casual category embraces a wide range of colors, but it favors the brightest and most playful. While guys in the category use lots of black and blue, they combine those darks with bright colors and pastels. Such vibrancy is unique to this category.

Young Professional/Modern Casual

This guy is *cool*. He displays an urban edge and has a penchant for all things "smooth." He takes his job very seriously, but he plays seriously too. He may work in a tech job, or be an aspiring rock star. He's probably in his mid-twenties to forties. He spends a good amount of time at the workplace (perhaps a home office) and he may still succumb to all-night gaming sessions as easily as an evening at a slick restaurant with martinis and tapas. This style

> The Modern Casual guy wants to project an exacting image—be it at play or at work—about himself.

category is typified by designers such as Armani, Versace, Dolce & Gabbana, Kenneth Cole, and Michael Kors, and retailers such as Banana Republic. The palette is based on muted tones, grays, tans, and black.

An essential component of Modern Casual is the concept of the "New Office," a semiformal mode of dress in which sweaters figure prominently. This concept has evolved in reaction to the "casual office" dress of the dot-com era. The casual office trend was intended to loosen up modes of corporate dress and culture, but instead was so ill-defined that it left men with absolutely no idea of what to wear to work. The essential qualities of New Office and Modern Casual dress are clean lines, a perfect fit, and quality construction. The clothes in this category possess the versatility to transition from situation to situation throughout the day and evening, from lunch with friends to a big presentation to a dinner date. The importance of sweaters in this category is based on their flexibility—a vest under a jacket, a sweater with a tie or in lieu of a jacket. The Modern Casual guy wants to project an exacting image—be it at play or at work—about himself.

> His sense of style has matured under the influences of propriety and decorum. He actually *has* a tailor.

Corporate/Traditional

This guy knows how to wear a suit. His sense of style has matured under the influences of propriety and decorum. He actually *has* a tailor. He can match a tie to a shirt, he knows when three pieces are just the thing, and he probably doesn't wear jeans. The Traditionalist is typically a

How Men Shop

According to menswear retailers, the buying approach most men prefer is to pick out an outfit on a mannequin and say, "I'll take that in a medium." Do not try to force this guy into a dressing room—or it will be Game Over.

classic businessman. His age bracket is hard to pin down, but he's often older. This guy is precise in every detail of his dress and his conduct. His goal is to command your respect and attention simply by walking into a room. He wants to purchase the perfect garment and be able to rely on it. The opposite of trendy, the Traditionalist wants his clothes to last a lifetime, if possible.

The colors of the Corporate/Traditional category include the classic shades of black, gray, navy, burgundy, and hunter green. There's a little Cary Grant in this guy: He's dashing and composed but he's witty and fun to be around. For this fellow, sweaters are part of his formal dress wardrobe—a V neck with trousers for dinner with a client or a semi-casual meal with his family. On weekends, the traditional man may incorporate sweaters into his wardrobe for outdoor and other active activities. The Corporate/Traditionalist style tends to come from family background and/or a deep-rooted respect for tradition and career.

> Make him a participant, not a victim. In other words, avoid the sweater inquisition!

How to Identify His Personal Style

Start the process of identifying his personal style by completing the Personal Style Worksheet (see page 11). Review the data collection methods that follow, record your answers, and see how they correlate to a style category.

The Approach—Information Gathering

As you embark on your fashion sleuthing, please keep in mind your goal of keeping him involved and interested. Make him a participant, not a victim. In other words, avoid the sweater inquisition! Remember, if he's not into the subject now, try broaching it another time. Perhaps a few short and well-timed consultations will yield more valuable information than a lengthy grilling session ever could. Here are few approaches to make his participation fairly painless, and maybe even fun.

■ **Let him diagnose himself.** Read through the personal style categories together (see page 6). Let him evaluate his own style. You may discover that although he dresses like a Traditionalist, he's a closet Active Casual guy and would really prefer a sporty "manly man" sweater over the V-necked vest you originally thought he'd like. He may just surprise you.

■ **Go shopping with him.** If he can stand it, take him shopping and ask him specific questions as you browse, such as "What do you think of this collar?" and "Do you like the stripes in this sweater?" Consider what you want to learn before you get to the store and keep your questions direct and pertinent. Use the Personal Style Worksheet as a guide. Yes, almost all men profess to absolutely hate shopping (if yours doesn't, count your blessings). Perhaps they feel that shopping is a waste of time and that

> Perhaps they feel that shopping is a waste of time and that they could be doing something "worthwhile," such as fixing the lawn mower or watching a football game.

they could be doing something "worthwhile," such as fixing the lawn mower or watching a football game. Shopping may also conjure up memories, real or imagined, of being dragged around department stores and

Personal Style Worksheet

Working with your guy, check, circle, or highlight the column that fits his M.O. When the worksheet is complete, the category that has the most responses is his predominant personal style category. Begin with that style category as the basis of your sweater project and further customize the garment from there.

	Young Men's/ Active Casual	Young Professional/ Modern Casual	Corporate/ Traditional
What is his age group?	Under 35	25–40	40 and up
His weekend clothes are____ as/from his weekday wardrobe.	The same	Different	Different
If he were to buy clothes, what labels would he choose?	Gap, J. Crew, Abercrombie & Fitch	Armani, D&G, Kenneth Cole, Banana Republic	Brooks Brothers, Bill Blass
What does he wear to work?	Jeans and a casual shirt	Sportshirt, closefit sweater, trousers	Suits
What colors dominate his wardrobe?	Brights, denim, plaids, pastels	Black, neutrals	Black, gray, navy, burgundy, hunter green
What is the dominant item in his wardrobe?	Jeans	Nice button-front shirts and trousers	Suits and dress shirts
When does he wear sweaters?	Every day	Work, play	Weekends, semiformal occasions
How does he like his sweaters to fit?	Big and roomy	Form fitting but comfortable	Trim and snug
What colors are the sweaters in his current wardrobe?	Bright or colorful	Black, camel, charcoal	Navy, green
What does he care about most when buying his clothes?	Color and trendiness	Fit and style	Longevity of wear
What are his preferred extracurricular activities?	Group sports, watching TV, going to the movies	Going to the new hot spot, listening to music	Sailing, visiting wineries, drinks at the club
What is his preferred drink?	Microbrews	Martini or another cocktail	Scotch or bourbon
How often does he buy new clothes?	Once a month	Every few months or twice a year	Only when something wears out
Does he change clothes for different events?	No	Depends	Yes

being embarrassed by their mothers. Remember how it felt as a preteen when your mom wouldn't let you pick out your own shoes or underwear? Fast-forward twenty years and that's most likely how he *still* feels about shopping. However, this time instead of Mom, it's his significant other inflicting the shopping misery.

Nonetheless, where he shops is a major indicator of his personal style. If he doesn't want to visit stores with you, make note of where he usually buys clothing. If you are going to a retail venue with him, make it fun, make it short, and let it be on his terms. When he's done, release him into the wilds of the electronics department, and enjoy picking out shoes for yourself in peace. If he doesn't hate the outing, maybe you can do it again in a month or so.

◼ **Show him images from catalogs.** This approach can be an easy way to peg his personal style. Tear out pictures of sweaters and garments you think he might like, or flip through the pages of a catalog or magazine together. If he likes a garment you show him, ask what he specifically likes about it. If he says he likes the setting, the activity shown, or the pants the model is wearing, maybe he is identifying with the image and feel of the catalog and not necessarily the garments. If pressed for more information as to why he likes a particular sweater, he may not have a good answer for you. If this is the case, make an assessment of the overall style of the catalog, magazine, or clothing line based on the personal style information previously presented. For example, are the models in their twenties, out of doors, and look like they just rolled out of bed? If so, Young Men's/ Active Casual is an easy verdict. If you are not confident

about your ability to assess the style of catalog, magazine, or clothing line correctly, show him images from the manufacturers and designers mentioned on the Personal Style Worksheet.

If he says he likes a specific sweater, thank your lucky stars! Your job just got a lot easier. His straightforward answer enables you to base your pattern choices on the garment depicted. However, if you are unable to get direct answers from him, be patient and observant. Just as when you're shopping, know in advance what you wish to ask. Use the Personal Style Worksheet as a guide. Try to ask specific questions about what he does or doesn't like about sweaters or other garments shown in the pictures. Your window of opportunity may be limited, so make these questions count. Above all, be sure to listen to him about what he wants to look like, and do not project your tastes onto him.

> If you are going to a retail venue with him, make it fun, make it short, and let it be on his terms. When he's done, release him into the wilds of the electronics department.

◼ **Evaluate his wardrobe.** Use this approach to enhance the information you have already collected or serve as a substitute if the other methods were a flop. Look at what clothes he wears most often, and ask him why. Evaluate the dominant colors in his closet and compare them to the colors of the three personal styles (see page 11). Use his existing wardrobe to answer the questions on the Personal Style Worksheet. Factor in his activities at work and at play, the magazines he reads, and the stores he patronizes. After you have compiled some information, ask him a few quick questions to confirm or

Personal Styles and Coordinating Designs

Young Men's/Active Casual	Young Professional/Modern Casual	Corporate/ Traditional
Basketcase Jacket	Basketcase Jacket	Basketcase Jacket
Cabled Rib Vest	Cabled Rib Cardigan	Cabled Rib Cardigan
Chain Link Pullover	Cabled Rib Vest	Cabled Rib Vest
Double Crossing Diamonds Aran Pullover	Chain Link Pullover	Classic Camel Vest
Fred's Jazz Vest	Classic Camel Vest	Hyland Argyle Vest
Garter Stitch Aran Cardigan	Double Crossing Diamonds Aran Pullover	Perpendicular Lines Pullover
Garter Stitch Aran Pullover	Fast Favorite Vest	Tweeds Cardigan
Jack's Aran Cardigan	Fred's Jazz Vest	
Jack's Aran Pullover	Garter Stitch Aran Cardigan	
Rustic Raglan Pullover	Garter Stitch Aran Pullover	
	Hyland Argyle Vest	
	Jack's Aran Cardigan	
	Perpendicular Lines Pullover	
	Tweeds Cardigan	

contradict your personal style assessment. If his answers don't jibe with your wardrobe evaluation, try the catalog approach again.

Choosing the Right Pattern from the Design Collection

For each design in the collection you will find a personal style classification. Some designs fall into more than one classification. The classifications will help you work through the synthesis of the right pattern, yarn, color, and sizing. You may wish to have your guy look through the entire collection and note his favorites, or show him the ones that correspond to his personal style category.

Now, let's move on to picking the right color and the right yarn for his custom sweater!

Chapter 3:

Selecting the Perfect Color and Fiber

Choosing and wearing the right color gives a guy a sense of confidence and harmony. The right color enhances his natural good looks and garners compliments. Many color analysis theories have been developed in the past twenty years; the most popular ones group people into seasonal categories and require them to carry a set of fabric swatches at all times to ensure that a spontaneous garment purchase falls within their personal palette. However, I don't know a lot of guys who will allow you to use the words "personal palette" around them, let alone admit that they could have one.

Ever wonder how men determine their color choices in clothing? They frequently base choices on their interpretation of corporate dress or other dictates of their work environment. Sometimes they simply reach for their favorite color. Or perhaps they pull on the color they've been wearing all their lives, ever since their mothers were picking out their clothes and dressing them. Later in life, what they wear switches from Mom's choice to the significant other's suggestions or purchases. But—and it's a big but—following any of these approaches when you're knitting a garment

for a man can lead to big trouble.

The notion of subscribing to a work uniform can quickly go awry. For lots of guys, a gray suit is a gray suit and he'll wear one every day if he thinks it conforms to the corporate norm. He'll continue to do so even if he knows the suit doesn't quite look right on him. In fact, this particular guy may look terrible in traditional corporate gray, and rather than attaining the power and authority he believes the suit will bring, he feels uncomfortable. His confidence and job performance may be affected. The simple realization that a navy blue suit (or sweater vest) would suit him better could do wonders for his career.

Favorite colors can also get a guy in trouble. Superbright royal purple is a very exciting color, but it may be best used for a set of towels rather than a handknitted sweater. Favorite colors can be an indication of what looks best on a guy (but not always), so consider using them as a starting point rather than the ultimate choice. Explore a range of shades and hues before making your selection.

Moms and significant others are another can of worms. Unfortunately, when we buy things for other people we are often buying what *we* like best or what *we* think will look good on them. Many times our judgment is clouded by our own favorite or flattering colors. When a mother is shopping for a child, she likely chooses gar-

> A guy can be stuck in a bad color rut established at the age of two.

ments in *her* favorite colors. A guy may get accustomed to these colors, since his mom always told him how great he looked in them. He can be stuck in a bad color rut established at the age of two.

Likewise, as knitters, we must take care when choosing colors and patterns for a man. Are we selecting something that will truly complement him? Or are we gravitating toward a project that is interesting to knit and features a new technique or flashy new yarn? This is where the tragedy of the one-wear-only sweater originates.

Let's break that cycle now! Making a good color selection requires a few intuitive, commonsense ideas. Apply the basic concepts below and a flattering garment is sure to follow. With the many compliments the wearer will undoubtedly receive, he'll shortly be asking you to make him another sweater!

To Select the Right Color:

■ Determine if his skin tone is warm or cool.

■ Use the dominant colors in his wardrobe and/or his favorite colors to guide you toward your selection.

■ Conduct a color test—monitor how a color makes him look and feel and whether he receives compliments while wearing it.

Determining Skin Tone

Most color analysis theories use skin tone as a cornerstone for color selection. The root of this idea lies in basic color theory and the color wheel. At the most rudimentary level, colors are divided into two categories: warm and cool. Warm colors are those that contain red and cool colors are those that contain blue. Generally, skin tones are either yellow-based (a color closer to red than blue and therefore warm) or blue-based (cool). So regardless of ethnicity, people with a yellow-based skin tone look best in warm colors; those with a blue-based skin tone look best in cool colors.

Color theory goes on to differentiate between a warm red and a cool red and who should wear which, as well as what shade of off-white is best for a person—ivory or oyster. Color theory can get very complex, and there

> Generally, skin tones are either yellow-based (a color closer to red than blue and therefore warm) or blue-based (cool).

are many professionals out there to help you if you want to investigate the topic further.

However, the bottom line for us in our quest to choose the right yarn color for our guy is this: Does a color enrich his skin tone or make him look dead? This is pretty straightforward, and you don't need an advanced degree in art or training in color analysis to figure it out. You just need a couple of minutes, your intuition, some samples of color, and a willing participant.

Skin Tone Test

Stand in natural light and look closely at your guy's face color. If he doesn't have a beard, do this when he is clean-shaven. If it is hard to detect his skin tone, or if he has a beard, look at the skin on the insides of his wrists or stomach. Does it appear yellowish or bluish? To isolate the area you are looking at and provide a neutral basis for comparison, hold a piece of white paper next to his skin. If he appears to have a warm skin tone, hold some warm-colored items near his face—yellow towels, an orange T-shirt, chocolate brown quilting fabric, a russet red throw pillow, whatever. Do these yellow/red-based colors make his skin glow, bring out the color in his eyes, and flatter his face, or do they make him look, well, dead? If dead is the answer, try again with shades complementary to blue because his skin tone is probably cool.

Color Test

Now, using his newly diagnosed skin tone as your guide, you are ready to choose the perfect color for his sweater. Following the basic rule of thumb that warm skin tones are best suited to warm colors and cool skin tones are best suited to cool colors, start playing around with various shades and intensities of colors. Remember that certain colors are typically associated with certain categories of dress. You may wish to keep his personal style type in mind

> A little patience can go a long way when the alternative is turning him off from the whole project for good.

while you make your color selections. As a reminder:

■ *Young Men's/Active Casual:* Bright colors and pastel shades.

■ *Young Professional/Modern Casual:* Neutrals and muted tones, tans, grays, and black.

■ *Corporate/Traditional:* Dark colors and shades that include black, gray, navy, burgundy, and hunter green.

Have your materials ready, and request five minutes when he'll be a willing participant. If he hedges or seems reluctant, do it another time. A little patience can go a long way when the alternative is turning him off from the

whole project for good.

Once he is ready for the color test, find a place with good natural light. Hold color samples up to his face and see if they pass the "not dead" test. Note whether a color accents his eyes. The right color will make his face glow, while the color itself recedes into the background.

> Do these yellow/red-based colors make his skin glow, bring out the color in his eyes, and flatter his face, or do they make him look, well, dead?

Use the colors already in his wardrobe as a sensible starting point for choosing your samples because he will most likely wear his new sweater with clothes he already owns. His wardrobe may reflect his favorite colors, as well as what he believes looks good on him. The good news here is that you don't need to deny him that royal purple; simply tone it down a bit. Experiment with shaded or muted purples—and remember that his warm skin tone needs a purple that features more red than blue. Conversely, select a blue purple for a cool skin tone.

Now you're really close to choosing the perfect color. His contribution thus far has been extremely important, not only because you can't make his perfect sweater without his help, but because he has been invited to participate in the entire process, allowing him a sense of involvement and ownership in the outcome.

Now it's time for a practice run. Ask him to wear the selected colors for a few days and make sure to solicit input from a wide variety of people so any of their individual color prejudices are ruled out. Using his skin tone, his color preferences, and the information gathered for understanding his personal style, ask him to wear garments in the top two color choices for a few days. These

items may include a T-shirt, a tie, a winter scarf, or a hat. Whatever it is, it should be the closest item to his face. Ask him to notice if these colors bring him compliments. How do these colors make him feel? Are his eyes more noticeable in one color than another? Has anyone asked him if he's gotten a haircut, or come right out and said, "That color looks great on you!"?

The *right* colors will focus attention on his face, make his eyes glow, even out his overall skin tone, and reduce shadows and lines. His face will brighten up and you will notice a sense of visual harmony.

The *wrong* colors will make his eyes recede, dominate his face, make shadows and imperfections more obvious, and cast a yellow or green tone on his skin (giving him the dreaded "dead look").

Choosing Fibers

Many guys I surveyed said that they like sweaters made of soft, easy-to-care-for materials. Comfort and warmth were also important considerations. The boom in the handknitting industry in recent years has provided knitters with amazing

> To avoid the itchies, consider using some of the fantastic fiber blends now available in handknitting yarns.

yarns in all price ranges. The combination of technological innovations with classic natural fibers means that there has never been a better time to be a knitter . . . or a *guy* who is about to receive a handknitted sweater. To find the perfect yarn, reflect on the following concerns.

The Itchy, Fuzzy, Heebie-Jeebies Dance

Is your guy sensitive? Sensitive to scratchy fabrics, that is. Can he wear natural fiber sweaters with just a T-shirt un-

derneath, or does he do the "itchy, fuzzy, heebie-jeebies dance" at the thought? If he's a heebie-jeebies guy, try a patch test with a few yarns to eliminate the biggest offenders. Visit your local yarn store or your personal stash, and place selected yarns under his chin or gently rub the yarn against his cheek. You'll know right away if a yarn doesn't pass the test. When he does get the itchies, he is most likely reacting to the long hairs characteristic of certain natural fibers, notably coarse wool and mohair. Ironically, long-haired fibers can give yarns great softness and amazing drape. To avoid the itchies, consider using some of the fantastic fiber blends now available in handknitting yarns. Look for cotton or cotton-blend yarns, blends of

> If you know that this guy will not put up with handwash/ air-dry-only instructions, head straight to the machine-washable yarns.

"offensive" fibers with soft ones—mohair with silk or alpaca with merino, for example—or famously soft fibers such as merino and cashmere.

Also check out machine-washable wools. The coarse cuticle of such wool has been altered to create a smoothed fiber capable of withstanding heat and washing in machines. Occasionally, people with wool sensitivities are actually reacting to the lanolin in the fiber, and machine-washable and scoured wools have had the lanolin removed. Thus they can be tolerated by people who believe they are in some way "allergic" to wool.

The Accidental Felt-Maker

Does he do his own laundering? Will he take the time to wash his sweaters properly in the gentle cycle or is he an accidental felt-maker? Will he properly air-dry a handknitted garment that cannot go in the dryer? Is it worth it to you to do it for him? If you know that this guy will not put up with hand-wash/air-dry-only instructions, head straight to the machine-washable yarns. Synthetic yarns are often considered the most durable options for washing. If you hold this point of view, I challenge you to expand your horizons.

Lucky knitters everywhere know that yarns of many fibers and blends have been added to the machine-washable category, most notably machine-washable wools, many of them made from super-soft merino. Lots of synthetic blends are currently on the market in all price ranges, with content ranging from 10 to 90-percent natural fibers. Check the label of the yarn and read the manufacturer's care instructions if you are not sure of a yarn's washability. Fully machine-washable products say so prominently on the label. On the other hand, I am of the belief that any yarn can be laundered in a washing machine if done so properly . . . but more on that later.

> You need to determine whether your guy wants a sweater for chilly outdoor activities, or if he dreads sweating to death at the office.

Another note: Just because a yarn is made of synthetic fibers does not mean it is fully machine washable. Rayons and some microfiber blends require special care akin to silk, so check those ball bands or ask your local yarn shop owner. One thing to keep in mind is that synthetics often produce much more vivid colors than natural fibers, so if you want a brighter look, consider the manmade or blended-fiber yarns first.

Climate Control

Let's state the obvious: Warmth is very important. So you need to determine whether your guy wants a sweater for chilly outdoor activities, or if he dreads sweating to death at the office. Think about his main activities: Is he active outside or indoors most of the day? Does he live in a warm or cool climate? If he wants to wear a sweater that won't give him heatstroke when he wears it indoors, consider a cotton or cotton-blend yarn.

While cotton yarns have a reputation for being heavy and saggy, cottons blended with either synthetic or animal fibers (such as wool or alpaca) offer a terrific alternative. The cotton component makes a sweater breathable and cools it down, while the synthetic or animal fiber gives the yarn buoyancy and creates a lighter knitted fabric. Moreover, sweaters knitted in these blended yarns are less apt to stretch and droop; the synthetic or animal fiber gives the yarn memory so it retains its shape when worn and laundered.

Your choice of garment style may factor in with this issue as much as fiber choice. If he gets hot easily and really wants a natural- or luxury-fiber sweater, consider knitting him a fine-gauge vest or an outerwear sweater. Stay away from heavy weight or bulky yarns, silk, 100-percent mohair, alpaca, and other longhaired fibers, as they are the warmest of all. Conversely, for the outdoorsman or weekend woodsman who wants to sport a rugged look, consider a big-gauge yarn made from warm woolies and beastly fur.

Caring for Handknits

Properly caring for a handknitted item is not as hard as you might think and, if done properly, will increase its lifespan. Keeping a natural fiber handknit away from chemical cleaning processes is a good idea. If your guy

can be mindful not to throw his sweater in with his jeans, but rather set it aside and wash it on its own, here are some guidelines for laundering sweaters and other handknits in the machine. (*Note:* This does not apply to front-loading machines.)

■ Use a mild detergent or a no-rinse wool wash.

Wool washes are great for natural fiber yarns that not have been treated for machine washability. The leading no-rinse wool-wash product currently on the market is Eucalan (see Resources, page 124). Check with your local yarn shop for other private-label products. Woolite is *not* a no-rinse wool wash and I don't recommend it for laundering handknits. Also note that no-rinse wool washes are not recommended for yarns that have been chemically treated to be machine washable. Wool washes usually contain lanolin or other conditioning agents to recondition fiber as it is washed, so they will gunk up machine-washable wools and synthetics.

> Whatever you do, do not let the washing machine agitate . . . or you'll be giving the sweater to the dog.

■ The most important factor in washing natural fiber handknits in the machine is to let them soak in cool water—absolutely under *no* circumstances agitate the garment or use hot water.

No-rinse wool wash makes this process easy. Simply fill up your top-loading washer on its low-water setting with cool water and stop the wash cycle. Add the wool wash, then add the sweater and let it soak. If the garment is very soiled, let it soak overnight. Then, manually advance the machine to the regular spin cycle and spin out all the excess water. Lay the garment flat on a towel or sweater drying rack and keep it away from sunlight. Re-shape the sweater to its proper size and shape, and leave it alone for a day or two, depending on the climate you live in. That's it!

If you are not using a no-rinse product and are laundering a natural fiber, proceed as above, using a very small amount of detergent. Let the sweater soak. Then run it through the spin cycle and refill the machine with clean water. Let the sweater soak again, then spin it out. If you did not use too much soap, that should do it. If the garment is still sudsy, repeat the rinse soak. Whatever you do, *do not* let the washing machine agitate . . . or you'll be giving the sweater to the dog. Dry as above.

■ For machine-washable fibers, most manufacturers suggest using the gentle or delicate/knits cycle. Add a small amount of mild detergent and let the machine do its thing. This is the easiest method of all. Check your ball band, because some machine-washable yarns state that they can be run through the dryer at a low-temperature setting. However, laying flat to dry is preferable to maintain the proper shape and size of the sweater you have worked so hard to customize.

Chapter 4:

Making It Fit, Making It a Favorite

The average Joe—have you ever met him? Is there such a thing as average, and can you use a set of average measurements and safely assume a sweater is going to look good on any guy? Most women are familiar with the notion of "average" body size and often go off the deep end to strive to meet this norm. Men just want to feel good in their clothes; racking up a few compliments along the way is an added bonus. A sane approach for us all is to understand how our body traits either comply with or differ from the sizing of garments, and to learn how to optimize what we've got and camouflage the rest. That way, we can bring the body's shape into an overall balance.

Body Types and Fit Issues

The "ideal male" body is proportioned with leg to torso length about equal, knuckles hanging about mid-body (at the height of the crotch when a man stands with slightly sloped shoulders).

There are three categories of typical men's body physiques:

■ *Athletic:* The shoulder is wider than the hip as the body tapers in toward the waist. This category also includes a square-shouldered guy.

■ *Typical:* The hip and shoulders are a similar width, and the body is straight from shoulder to waist.

■ *Full:* The hip is wider than the shoulder.

Each of these physiques also includes the traits of tall, thin, and short. So you may have a guy with the proportions of the Typical category, but he is six feet four inches tall, with a full-barreled chest. And he isn't necessarily thin. To better understand a man's specific fit needs, you should assess the following body components. Make careful measurements, as follows, and use the Perfect Fit Worksheet to record them. Then use the suggested fit solutions to pick the perfect pattern and make the necessary customizations.

Height

Measure his height with his back straight against a wall, barefoot with feet together against the join of wall and floor (much like when your parents checked your height on a growth chart). Mark his height on the wall with a pencil and measure it later with a tape measure. The average Joe is between five feet nine inches and six feet tall. If he is over six feet, he's a "tall." If he's less than five feet eight inches, he's a "short."

Chest

Measure his chest circumference just under the arms. Divide this number by two to determine chest width. Find his favorite sweater that most resembles the one you want to make (i.e., pullover, cardigan, vest), one whose fit he appreciates. Measure the width at the underarm. The difference between his body measurement and the garment measurement is his preferred amount of ease.

Short-Waisted or Long Torso

Determine the length of his legs by measuring up from the floor to his hip joint, where the body bends as the knee is raised. If his legs are longer than the rest of his body, he is short-waisted, and if they are shorter, he has a long torso.

Arms

Ask him to stand up straight but comfortably. Notice if his arms hang at, above, or below his crotch. If his arms hang at this point, they are average length; above, they are short; below, they are long. Then measure the length of each arm from the ball of his shoulder joint to the longest fingertip and from the ball of his shoulder to his wrist. One arm may be longer than the other, so make a note of which and by how much.

Shoulder Slope

Assess whether his shoulders appear to be square, slightly sloped, or rounded and very sloped. Shoulder slope can

Shortcut to a Good Fit

Find a sweatshirt, fleece pullover, or sweater that you both agree fits him well. Measure the width of the chest at the underarm (A), the shoulders (B), neck opening (C), total length (D), and sleeve length (E). Use these measurements as a key when you are selecting the right size to knit, and customize the sweater you knit him to match these dimensions.

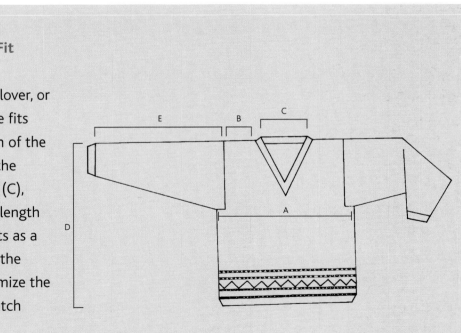

affect how the sleeves hang and whether sleeve length adjustments need to be made.

Short or Long Neck

This measurement is determined more by the fit of his clothes and his collar preference than by a tape measure. If his neck is full or he has a thick or double chin, he is considered short-necked. If his shoulders slope noticeably or his Adam's apple protrudes, he's long-necked.

Solutions and Customizations for Great Fit

When customizing a sweater for your guy, talk to him and be particularly sensitive about physical attributes he may want to accentuate or de-emphasize. Keep these in mind when choosing from the customization options given here. For example, if he's been working hard at the gym to develop broad shoulders, you may not want to choose a style option that downplays them.

Physique

If his physique is **Athletic**, he will most likely have wide shoulders. Just as you would do for a square-shouldered guy, use V necks to point attention away from the upper body and perhaps raglan sleeves to reduce shoulder bulk. Use vests to visually reduce shoulder width and focus the eye toward the center of the body.

Design recommendations: All V-neck designs, Cabled Rib Cardigan, Cabled Rib Vest, Fred's Jazz Vest, Rustic Raglan Pullover

If his physique is **Average**, nearly everything looks good on him. Use his body measurements as a guide, and customize the garment and sleeve length for the ultimate fit.

If his physique is **Full**, use vertical lines and solid colors to suggest length. Stay away from bulky yarns and pronounced ribbings that will emphasize the midriff. A V neck may also add a slimming effect. Consider a bright shade for his sweater so he can pair it with dark pants to de-emphasize the middle.

The "Perfect" Size

You've probably heard of "sample size 6," but do you know what it means in terms of how clothes fit you? For garment manufacturers, sample size refers to a set of measurements that may or may not be based on a typical body type. Once the sample garment is made, the rest of the sizes are "graded"—made bigger or smaller—on a percentage system. By the time the sample size 6, or Men's Medium, is graded up to a 14, or X-Large, it may have lost much of its resemblance to the original garment and much of the nuance and fit of the prototype. In addition, sample sizes are not standard either, which is why one line may be referred to as having a more "generous cut" than another, and why garments of the same size from different designers may fit very differently. For this reason, once you find a designer whose sizing fits you well, you may decide to become a loyal customer.

Perfect Fit Worksheet

Photocopy this worksheet and follow the directions and guidelines in this chapter to record your guy's measurements. Make sure to recheck his measurements when you start a new project, as he may have grown or gained/lost weight.

Date: _____

Name of recipient: _____ Age: _____

Height: _____

He is: ☐ Tall ☐ Thin ☐ Short

Leg length from floor to hip: _____ Torso length (height minus leg length): _____

☐ Torso length is more than leg length—he has a **Long Torso**

☐ Leg Length is more than Torso Length—he is **Short-Waisted**

Chest circumference: _____ Chest width: _____

Preferred amount of ease: _____

Arm length from shoulder to wrist: _____

Left arm: _____ Right arm: _____ He likes his cuff _____" below wrist joint

Shoulder Slope is ☐ Square ☐ Slight ☐ Average ☐ Rounded

Neck is ☐ Long ☐ Short

His Physical Type is:

☐ **Athletic:** The shoulder is wider than the hip as the body tapers in toward the waist.

☐ **Typical:** The hip and shoulders are a similar width, and the body is straight from shoulder to waist.

☐ **Full:** The hip is wider than the shoulder.

His Fit Issues and Solutions   **Your Choice of Fit**

_____   _____

_____   _____

_____   _____

_____   _____

Design recommendations: Cabled Rib Cardigan, Cabled Rib Vest, Classic Camel Vest, Double Crossing Diamonds Aran Pullover, Fast Favorite Vest, Garter Stitch Aran Cardigan, Garter Stitch Aran Pullover

Height

If he is **Short**, use vertical lines to add height. Ribbed sweaters or sweaters featuring vertical panels are recommended.

> Assess his chest in relation to the rest of his body. If he is wide at the shoulders and/or barrel-chested, stay away from motifs or horizontal lines that will draw attention to this area.

Design recommendations: Cabled Rib Cardigan, Cabled Rib Vest, Double Crossing Diamonds Aran Pullover, Fast Favorite Vest, Garter Stitch Aran Cardigan, Garter Stitch Aran Pullover, Jack's Aran Cardigan, Jack's Aran Pullover

If he is **Tall**, bulkiness and horizontal lines will de-emphasize height. Making a dark-colored sweater to be worn with lighter colored pants will also minimize height.

Design recommendations: Basketcase Jacket, Fred's Jazz Vest, Jack's Aran Cardigan, Jack's Aran Pullover, Perpendicular Lines Pullover, Rustic Raglan Pullover

Chest

Assess his chest in relation to the rest of his body. If he is wide at the shoulders and/or barrel-chested, stay away from motifs or horizontal lines that will draw attention to this area. Also consider V necks to focus attention downward.

Design recommendations: Classic Camel Vest, Perpendicular Lines Pullover, Tweeds Cardigan

Short-Waisted or Long Torso

If he is **Short-waisted**, draw the eye down with a long length below the armhole. Reduce or eliminate ribbing to remove lines across the body and visually lower the belt-line. Use vertical lines to emphasize length.

Design recommendations: Cabled Rib Cardigan, Cabled Rib Vest, Chain Link Pullover, Double Crossing Diamonds Aran Pullover, Garter Stitch Aran Cardigan, Garter Stitch Aran Pullover, Tweeds Cardigan

If he has a **Long Torso**, raise his belt-line by shortening the length of the body below the armhole. This shortening can be done with any design.

Arms

If his arms are **Short**, pay particular attention to how far

---

Knitting for Boys

The main recommendation I can offer here is to make it big! Use the dimensions and style features of popular or favorite clothing manufacturers as your guide. He will grow—it is inevitable—and you want him to wear his sweater for a long time. Also, current boys' trends have taken a "bigger is better" stance. Keep versatility in mind and consider letting his sweater be something he's allowed to wear all the time in place of a jean jacket or fleece pullover.

the drop shoulder of the garment falls below the natural shoulder line. A wide shoulder will visually shorten the arm and physically drop the sleeve, so consider a sweater that uses the indented drop shoulder. With all sleeves, customization is key. If arms are different lengths, tailor them accordingly. If he is going to wear a shirt under his sweater, a longer sleeve will show less cuff and create a longer visual line.

Design recommendations: All vests, Cabled Rib Cardigan, Chain Link Pullover, Perpendicular Lines Pullover, Tweeds Cardigan

> If sleeves become a really tricky issue, consider knitting a vest. You will eliminate a big headache for yourself now and later.

If his arms are **Long**, utilize the top-down sleeve technique featured in this design collection to its fullest! Add the necessary length to any design at or before the cuff. This method allows your guy to try the sweater on as it is being knitted and ensures the best results.

If sleeves become a really tricky issue, consider knitting a vest. You will eliminate a big headache for yourself now and later.

Shoulder Slope

If his shoulders are very **Broad** or **Square**, consider raglan sleeves and V necks to point attention away from the upper body. Vests are great for broad or square shoulders—they reduce shoulder width and the contrast in color and texture at the shoulder draws the eye toward the center of the body.

Design recommendations: Cabled Rib Vest, Fast Favorite Vest, Fred's Jazz Vest, Hyland Argyle Vest, Rustic Raglan Pullover

If his shoulders have **Major Slope** or are **Rounded**, use horizontal lines for straightening and camouflage. Avoid sweaters with thick waist ribbings that will puff or blouse and accentuate sloped or rounded shoulders.

Design recommendations: Cabled Rib Cardigan, Cabled Rib Vest, Double Crossing Diamonds Aran Pullover, Fast Favorite Vest, Fred's Jazz Vest, Garter Stitch Aran Cardigan, Garter Stitch Aran Pullover

Short or Long Neck

If his neck is **Short**, visually create length with V necks or downward emphasis at the neckline. Shallow crewnecks can also appear to add length.

Design recommendations: All V-neck designs, Chain Link Pullover, Garter Stitch Aran Cardigan, Garter Stitch Aran Pullover

If his neck is **Long**, consider turtlenecks or mock turtlenecks, either by choosing a turtleneck design or customizing the length of the neck treatment.

Design recommendations: Double Crossing Diamonds Aran Pullover, Jack's Aran Pullover, Rustic Raglan Pullover

Customization Tips

To lengthen or shorten the body before you knit the armhole: Determine the desired total length. This length may be based on body measurements or fit issues, or on the total length of a favorite, well-fitting sweater or sweatshirt. Look at the pattern schematic and find the armhole depth for your size. Subtract armhole depth from the total length. The remainder is the length you need to work for the body before you knit the armhole. Work even for this length in the pattern as set. Then proceed with the armhole shaping and the rest of the pattern as directed.

Sleeves: The sweaters in the design collection feature drop shoulder or modified drop shoulder sleeves and a top-down technique. Use this feature to its fullest to customize sleeve length. Stitches for the sleeve are picked up at the armhole and knitted down, decreasing as you go. This technique will allow your guy to try the sweater on as it is being knitted, ensuring that it fits to a tee.

Plotting Out the Sleeve: To properly understand how the sleeve will fit, and where the drop shoulder will fall, measure the sweater size against his body, with attention to the width of the shoulder. Look at the sweater schematic. From his spine, measure out the width of the garment's shoulder, plus one half the back neck width. This is the point where the top of the sleeve will join the shoulder. It will fall below the natural shoulder, and sleeve length measurements should start here. If the sleeve from the size that best fits his body hangs too long, consider choosing a modified drop shoulder design or customizing the pattern to include this feature. A modified drop shoulder occurs when an indentation has been made on the shoulder and an extension, equal to the indentation, is knitted at the top of the sleeve. This extension is not included in the measurement of the sleeve, because it is theoretically part of the width of the body. The effect is a shoulder line that has been raised without the trouble of a set-in sleeve. The drop shoulder also allows you to knit the sleeve out from the body from the top down and sew the extension into place after completing the knitting (see page 124).

> Have your guy try on the sweater as you knit the sleeve. Together, determine the perfect place for the sleeve to end. To lengthen, just keep knitting!

Modifying a drop shoulder sweater: This is best done with a design that does not have any cable patterning or complexities along the shoulder edge. Based on the measurements you have taken, determine by how much you want to raise the shoulder seam in toward the body. Multiply this amount by the number of stitches per inch for your gauge. When it's time to shape the armhole, bind off this number of stitches, in addition to the number specified in the pattern. When you're knitting the sleeve, pick up your sleeve stitches at the shoulder between these deep notches and leave the bound-off stitches free. Add an extension equal to your indentation to the top of the sleeve—you can do this visually by knitting until it is as long as the notch is deep—and then begin decreasing for your sleeve shaping as directed in the pattern. If you have chosen a modified drop shoulder pattern and wish to indent it further, remember that there is already an extension at the top of the sleeve to which you will be adding. Using the visual method takes the thinking out of this step (and knitters can't help but over-think what they are doing most of the time!).

> Do not discount the power of the vest; it can even restore domestic harmony!

If you need a longer sleeve: Two words: easy peasy! Have your guy try on the sweater as you knit the sleeve. Together, determine the perfect place for the sleeve to end. To lengthen, just keep knitting! If your sleeve has a ribbing, knit the extra length in pattern stitch before the ribbing, or lengthen the ribbing. If your pattern does not have a ribbing or sleeve treatment, continue to knit even in pattern to the desired length.

If you need a shorter sleeve: Pick up the number of stitches as indicated for your size, but follow the decrease

instructions for the next size smaller sleeve. When you have worked to 1" before the beginning of the cuff, evaluate the fit of the lower sleeve. If it's too wide, work a few more decrease rows, or decrease the required number of stitches evenly in the final row above the cuff.

Remember, this is *supposed to be fun*. As mentioned above, if the sleeve issue becomes overly daunting or a flat-out nightmare, how about knitting a vest? Vests are very versatile, stylish, and currently popular in fashion trends. Do not discount the power of the vest; it can even restore domestic harmony!

Choosing the Pattern and Making It Fit

The sweaters in the *Men in Knits* collection have been developed with versatility and ease of customization in mind. They feature drop shoulders for easy fit, easy construction, and easy sleeve alteration. The vests range from traditional and dressy to loose and casual.

You have now identified your guy's body type and fit issues, and reviewed the suggested design solutions and customization tips. You have discovered his personal style and learned what kind of sweater he wants and why. Together, you have selected the perfect color and ideal yarn. Lastly, you have profiled his body type, found solutions to his particular fit issues, and determined just the right design for him.

Cheerful knitting! Here's to the perfect sweater he'll actually wear!

Fit Issues and Corresponding Design Recommendations

Athletic Physique	All V-Neck Designs
	Cabled Rib Cardigan
	Cabled Rib Vest
	Fred's Jazz Vest
	Rustic Raglan Pullover
Average Physique	All Designs
Full Physique	Cabled Rib Cardigan
	Cabled Rib Vest
	Classic Camel Vest
	Double Crossing Diamonds Aran Pullover
	Fast Favorite Vest
	Garter Stitch Aran Cardigan
	Garter Stitch Aran Pullover
Height—Short	Cabled Rib Cardigan
	Cabled Rib Vest
	Double Crossing Diamonds Aran Pullover
	Fast Favorite Vest
	Garter Stitch Aran Cardigan
	Garter Stitch Aran Pullover
	Jack's Aran Cardigan
	Jack's Aran Pullover
Height—Tall	Basketcase Jacket
	Fred's Jazz Vest
	Jack's Aran Cardigan
	Jack's Aran Pullover
	Perpendicular Lines Pullover
	Rustic Raglan Pullover
Thin	All Bulky Designs:
	Basketcase Jacket
	Jack's Aran Cardigan
	Jack's Aran Pullover
Barrel/Wide Chest	Classic Camel Vest
	Perpendicular Lines Pullover
	Tweeds Cardigan

Short Waist	Cabled Rib Cardigan Cabled Rib Vest Chain Link Pullover Double Crossing Diamonds Aran Pullover Garter Stitch Aran Cardigan Garter Stitch Aran Pullover Tweeds Cardigan
Long Torso	Cabled Rib Cardigan Jack's Aran Pullover Perpendicular Lines Pullover
Broad Shoulders	Cabled Rib Vest Fast Favorite Vest Fred's Jazz Vest Hyland Argyle Vest Rustic Raglan Pullover
Round Shoulders	Cabled Rib Cardigan Cabled Rib Vest Double Crossing Diamonds Aran Pullover Fast Favorite Vest Fred's Jazz Vest Garter Stitch Aran Cardigan Garter Stitch Aran Pullover
Short Neck	All V-Neck Designs Chain Link Pullover Garter Stitch Aran Cardigan Garter Stitch Aran Pullover
Long Neck	Double Crossing Diamonds Aran Pullover Jack's Aran Pullover Rustic Raglan Pullover

Short Arms	All Vests
	Modified Shoulder Designs:
	    Cabled Rib Cardigan
	    Chain Link Pullover
	    Perpendicular Lines Pullover
	    Tweeds Cardigan

Part Two:

The Design Collection

Double Crossing Diamonds Aran Pullover

Here's a sweater that moves easily in both dressy and casual circles. An easy-care and lightweight cotton-blend yarn makes it soft and versatile. The cables offer a good challenge for a knitter new to the technique or a fun project for the seasoned Aran knitter. The pullover features body-lengthening vertical cable panels, a straight silhouette with no ribbing, and a rolled mock turtleneck that can be easily customized into a conventional crew neckband by working a shorter ribbing. This is a great pattern for all Personal Style categories. Choose this pattern for the following fit issues: *Full physique, Short, Short-Waisted,* and *Round Shoulders. Note:* This design is an adult version of the child's sweater that appeared in the Spring 2001 issue of *Interweave Knits,* available from tarahandknitting.com.

SPECIFICATIONS

Finished Sizes	Yarn	Needles	Notions	Gauge
Adult S (M, L, XL). 42 (45, 50, 54)" (106.5 [114.5, 127, 137] cm) finished chest. 24 (25, 26, 28)" (61 [63.5, 66, 71] cm) finished length. Sweater shown in size L.	Cascade Yarns Sierra (80% pima cotton, 20% wool; 191 yds [175 m]/100 g): #08 green, 8 (9, 10, 11) skeins.	Size 7 (4.5 mm): straight or 29" (70-cm) circular (circ). Size 5 (3.75 mm): 16" (40-cm) circ. Adjust needle size if necessary to obtain the correct gauge.	Stitch markers; stitch holders; darning needle; cable needle (cn); scissors; measuring tape; crochet hook G (4.5 mm) for picking up stitches (optional).	Using larger needles, 18 sts and 29 rows = 4" (10 cm) in seed stitch (seed st); 101 sts of entire double crossing diamond panel from chart = 17¾" (45 cm) wide; 37 sts from section of chart used for sleeves = 7¼" (18.5 cm) wide. Check your gauge before you begin.

Seed Stitch (seed st)

Row 1: *K1, p1; repeat from *, ending k1 if there is an odd number of sts.

Row 2 and all following rows: Purl the knit sts, and knit the purl sts as they appear.

Bobble: P1, k1 through back loop (tbl), p1, k1 tbl all in same st, then pass first 3 sts made over last st to decrease back to 1 st.

Back

With larger needles, loosely CO 115 (123, 133, 143) sts. Set up patterns as follows, placing markers where indicated if desired: (RS) Work 7 (11, 16, 21) sts in seed

st, work center 101 sts according to Row 1 of double crossing diamond chart, omitting bobbles on this row *only*, work 7 (11, 16, 21) sts in seed st. *Note:* The number of rows required to work each element of the cable chart varies; for each pattern section, repeat the rows indicated by the red boxes (row numbers shown for rows 1–12 only). Work even in patterns as established, maintaining sts at each side in seed st, until piece measures 13 (14, 14, 15½)" (33 [35.5, 35.5, 39.5] cm) from the beginning, ending with a WS row. Armhole shaping: BO 4 sts at beg of next 2 rows—107 (115, 125, 135) sts. Work even in patterns until piece measures 23½ (24½, 25½, 27½)" (59.5 [62, 65, 70] cm) from beginning, ending with a WS row. Shape back neck: Work 31 (35, 38, 42) sts in pattern, join new ball of yarn, BO center 45 (45, 49, 51) sts, work in pattern to end. Working each side separately, work even in pattern until piece measures 24 (25, 26, 28)" (61 [63.5, 66, 71] cm) from beginning. Place 31 (35, 38, 42) sts for each shoulder on separate holders.

Front

Work as for back until piece measures 21 (22, 23, 25)" (53.5 [56, 58.5, 63.5] cm) from beginning, ending with a WS row. Shape front neck: Work 43 (47, 52, 57) sts in pattern, join new ball of yarn, BO center 21 sts (center diamond section of chart), work in pattern to end. Working each side separately, decrease 1 st at each neck edge every row 3 (3, 7, 9) times, then every other row 9 (9, 7, 6)

times—31 (35, 38, 42) sts at each side. Work even in pattern until piece measures 24 (25, 26, 28)" (61 [63.5, 66, 71] cm) from beginning. Place 31 (35, 38, 42) sts for each shoulder on separate holders.

Sleeves

Matching right front and back shoulders, with right sides of fabric held together, join right shoulder using three-needle bind-off technique. Repeat for left shoulder. With RS facing, using larger needles, beginning at inner corner of armhole notch, pick up and knit 103 (103, 113, 117) sts evenly from one armhole notch to the other (using crochet hook for assistance, if desired). Set up patterns as follows, placing markers where indicated if desired: (WS) Work 33 (33, 38, 40) sts in seed st, pm, k4, p2, k2, pm, k8, p2, k1, p2, k8, pm, k2, p2, k4, pm, work 33 (33, 38, 40) sts in seed st. On the next row (RS), work 33 (33, 38, 40) sts

Double Crossing Diamonds

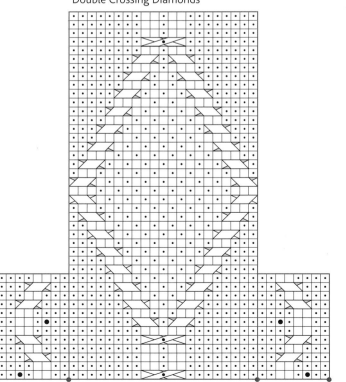

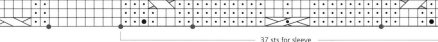

37 sts for sleeve

*Note: Do not work bobbles on the first row of each piece; do work bobbles where indicated on subsequent rows.

in seed st, work Row 1 of center 37-st section from chart as indicated for sleeve, omitting bobbles on this row *only,* work 33 (33, 38, 40) sts in seed st. Work even in patterns as established for 5 more rows, ending with a WS row. Shape sleeve: Continue in patterns, and beginning with the next RS row, decrease 1 st at each side every 4 rows 6 (6, 17, 24) times, then every 5 rows 19 (19, 11, 6) times— 53 (53, 57, 57) sts. Work even in patterns until piece measures 18¼ (18¼, 18¾, 19¼)" (46.5 [46.5, 47.5, 49] cm from pickup row, or ¾" (2 cm) less than desired length, ending with a WS row. Change to smaller needle, and work in St st for 1½" (3.8 cm). BO all sts loosely. St st edging will roll up to about ¾" (2 cm) long for a finished sleeve length of 19 (19, 19½, 20)" (48.5 [48.5, 49.5, 51] cm.

Finishing

Lightly steam block only if needed; blocking can compromise the rich texture of the knitting you have worked so hard to achieve. Sew sleeve and side seams, reversing the seam for the rolled edges of sleeves so RS of seam will show when purl side of St st rolls to the outside of garment. Weave in ends.

Neckband

With smaller needle and RS facing, and beginning at left shoulder seam, pick up and knit 76 (76, 82, 88) sts evenly around neck opening as follows (using crochet hook for assistance, if desired): 12 (12, 14, 16) sts along side of left front neck, 18 sts across sts bound off at center front, 12 (12, 14, 16) sts along side of right front neck, 34 (34, 36, 38) sts across back neck. Join for working in the round (rnd), and pm to indicate beginning of rnd. Work in St st for 2" (5 cm), or desired length of neckband. BO all sts loosely as if to knit on next rnd. Weave in ends. *Note:* For a more conventional neckband, work in k1, p1 rib for 1" (2.5 cm) instead of rolled St st edge.

☐	knit on RS; purl on WS
·	purl on RS; knit on WS
●	bobble
☐	pattern repeat
●	marker (optional)
	sl 2 to cn, hold in front, k2, p1 from cn
	sl 1 to cn, hold in back, k2, p1 from cn
	sl 2 to cn, hold in front, k2, k1 from cn
	sl 1 to cn, hold in back, k2, k1 from cn
	sl 2 to cn, hold in front, k2, k2 from cn
	sl 2 to cn, hold in back, k2, k2 from cn
	sl 3 to cn, hold in back, k2, p last st on cn, k2 from cn

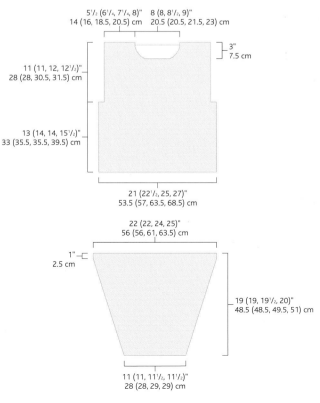

Jack's Aran

THE THREE SWEATERS in this group—adult pullover, child's pullover, and adult cardigan—share classic Aran panel design, a bulky quick knitting gauge, and the lattice stitch motif. The pullover features soft alpaca-blend yarn in solid colors for a casual, classic look. The cardigan, knit in a contemporary tweed yarn for a slightly more rustic flavor, is extremely versatile, replacing a jacket at the office and moving right into the weekend with its "cabin in the woods" feel. The rolled edges at the bottom band, cuffs, and neck of this design group add a modern flair to a classic silhouette.

Jack's Aran Cardigan

❧

This cardigan version of the Jack's Aran Pullover appeals to the Young Men's/Active Casual and Young Professional/Modern Casual guy, as well as the Corporate/Traditional man (if he's in a dress-down mood). Its rich cablework is intensified by a robust tweed in a classic shade of green. V-necked and sturdy, the sweater features contemporary fit and styling, and can be paired with either jeans or a tie. Consider making it an alternative to a coat. This sweater is another perfect choice for your burly (or wannabe burly) guy. Like the pullover version, Jack's Aran Cardigan is a good choice for the following fit issues: *Athletic and Average physiques, Long Neck, Tall, Thin.*

SPECIFICATIONS

Finished Sizes	Yarn	Needles	Notions	Gauge
Adult S/M (L, XL). 45 (51, 55)" (114.5 [129.5, 139.5] cm) finished chest. 24 (25³/₄, 27¹/₂)" (61 [65.5, 70] cm) finished length. Sweater shown in size S/M.	Classic Elite Gatsby (70% wool, 15% viscose, 15% nylon; 94 yds [86 m]/100 g): #2150 olive, 13 (15, 17) skeins.	Size 10 (6 mm): straight or 29" (70-cm) circular (circ). Size 9 (5.5 mm): straight or 29" (70-cm) circ. Adjust needle size if necessary to obtain the correct gauge.	Stitch markers; stitch holders; darning needle; cable needle (cn); scissors; measuring tape; five 1-inch (2.5-cm) buttons (shown: One World Button Supply NP 356-28 HBT Horn with Burnt Ring 28 mm), crochet hook J (6 mm) for picking up stitches (optional).	Using larger needles, 12 sts and 20 rows = 4" (10 cm) in seed stitch (seed st); 40 sts lattice and cable pattern from chart measure approximately 9" (23 cm) wide; 8 sts of sleeve cable from chart measure approximately 2" (5 cm) wide. Check your gauge before you begin.

Seed Stitch (seed st)

Row 1: *K1, p1; repeat from *, ending k1 if there is an odd number of sts.

Row 2 and all following rows: Purl the knit sts, and knit the purl sts as they appear.

Back

With smaller needles, CO 86 (94, 98) sts. Work in Stockinette stitch (St st) for 6 rows, or desired length of rolled edge, ending with a WS row, and increasing 8 sts evenly in last row—94 (102, 106) sts. On the next

row (RS), change to k2, p2 rib, beginning and ending the row with k2, and work in rib for 2" (5 cm), ending with a WS row and increasing 0 (0, 2) sts on last row—94 (102, 108) sts. Change to larger needles. On the next row (RS), work 3 (5, 7) sts seed st, work 40 sts from Row 1 of lattice and cable chart, work 8 (12, 14) sts seed st, work 40 sts from Row 1 of lattice and cable chart, work 3 (5, 7) sts seed st. Work even in patterns as established until piece measures 12½ (14¼, 15½)" (31.5 [36, 39.5] cm) with bottom edge rolled up, ending with a WS row. Armhole shaping: BO 2 sts at beg of next 2 rows—90 (98, 104) sts. Work even in patterns until piece measures 23½ (25¼, 27)" (59.5 [64, 68.5] cm) with bottom edge rolled up, ending with a WS row. Shape back neck: Work 32 (36, 39) sts in patterns, join new ball of yarn, BO center 26 sts, work in patterns to end. (*Note:* Although the same number of sts is bound off across the back neck for all sizes, the sts have different proportions of seed and cable patterns for each size, resulting in different back neck width measurements, as

shown on schematic.) Working each side separately, work even in patterns until piece measures 24 (25¾, 27½)" (61 [65.5, 70] cm) with bottom edge rolled up, and ending with a non-cabling (WS) row. Place 32 (36, 39) sts for each shoulder on separate holders.

Left Front

With smaller needles, CO 43 (47, 49) sts. Work in St st for 6 rows, or desired length of rolled edge, ending with a WS row, and increasing 4 sts evenly in last row—47 (51, 53) sts. On the next row (RS), establish k2, p2 rib as follows: *K2, p2; repeat from * to last 3 (3, 1) st(s), end k3 (3, 1). Work in rib as established for 2" (5 cm), ending with a WS row, and increasing 0 (0, 1) st on last row—47 (51, 54) sts. Change to larger needles. On the next row (RS), work 3 (5, 7) sts seed st, work 40 sts from Row 1 of lattice and cable chart, work 4 (6, 7) sts seed st. Work even in patterns as established until piece measures 12½ (14¼, 15½)" (31.5 [36, 39.5] cm) with bottom edge rolled up,

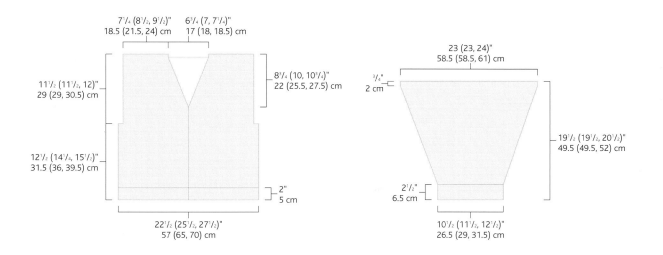

ending with a WS row. Armhole shaping: BO 2 sts at beg of next RS row—45 (49, 52) sts. Continue in patterns until piece measures 15¼ (15¾, 16¾)" (38.5 [40, 42.5] cm) from beginning, ending with a WS row. Shape V neck: Beginning with the next RS row, decrease 1 st at neck edge (end of RS rows or beginning of WS rows) every 3 rows 11 (5, 1) time(s), then every 4 rows 2 (8, 12) times—32 (36, 39) sts. Work even until piece measures 24 (25¾, 27½)" (61 [65.5, 70] cm) with bottom edge rolled up, and ending with a non-cabling (WS) row. Place sts on holder.

Right Front

With smaller needles, CO 43 (47, 49) sts. Work in St st for 6 rows, or desired length of rolled edge, ending with

a WS row, and increasing 4 sts evenly in last row—47 (51, 53) sts. On the next row (RS), establish k2, p2 rib as follows: K1 (3, 3), *p2, k2; repeat from * to end. Work in rib as established for 2" (5 cm), ending with a WS row, and increasing 0 (0, 1) st on last row—47 (51, 54) sts. Change to larger needles. On the next row (RS), work 4 (6, 7) sts seed st, work 40 sts from Row 1 of lattice and cable chart, work 3 (5, 7) sts seed st. Work even in patterns as established until piece measures 12½ (14¼, 15½)" (31.5 [36, 39.5] cm) with bottom edge rolled up, ending with a RS row. Complete as for left front, reversing shaping by binding off for armhole at the beginning of a WS row, and working V-neck shaping at the beginning of RS rows or end of WS rows. Place sts on holder as for left front.

Sleeves

Matching right front and back shoulders, with right sides of fabric held together, join right shoulder using three-needle bind-off technique. Repeat for left shoulder. With RS facing, using larger needles, beginning at inner corner of armhole notch, pick up and knit 72 (72, 74) sts evenly from one armhole notch to the other (using crochet hook for assistance, if desired). On the next row (WS), work as follows, pm between st panels where indicated, if desired: Work 32 (32, 33) sts seed st, pm, k2,

	knit on RS; purl on WS
	purl on RS; knit on WS
	sl 2 sts to cn and hold in back k2, k2 from cn
	sl 2 sts to cn and hold in front, k2, k2 from cn
	sl 2 st to cn and hold in back k2, p2 from cn
	sl 2 sts to cn and hold in front, p2, k2 from cn

Lattice and Cable

Sleeve Cable

p4, k2, pm, work 32 (32, 33) sts seed st. On the next row (RS), work as follows: 32 (32, 33) sts seed st, 8 sts from Row 1 of sleeve cable chart, 32 (32, 33) sts seed st. Work 3 rows even in patterns, ending with a WS row. Shape sleeve: Continue in patterns, and beginning with the next RS row, decrease 1 st at each side every 6 rows 1 (3, 8) time(s), then every 4 rows 18 (15, 9) times—34 (36, 40) sts. Work even until piece measures 17 (17, 18)" (43 [43, 45.5] cm) from pickup row, or 2½" (6.5 cm) less than desired length, ending with a WS row, and decreasing 0 (2, 2) sts evenly across in last row—34 (34, 38) sts. Change to smaller needles. Work in k2, p2 rib as for back for 2" (5 cm), ending with a WS row. On the next row (RS), knit across all sts. Change to smaller needles and work even in St st for 6 rows. BO all sts loosely.

Finishing

Lightly steam block only if needed; blocking can compromise the rich texture of the knitting you have worked so hard to achieve. Sew sleeve and side seams, reversing the seam for the rolled edges so RS of seam will show when purl side of St st sections rolls to the outside of garment. Weave in ends.

Front Band

Mark positions on left front for five evenly spaced buttonholes, the lowest located ½" (1.3 cm) up from bottom edge, and the highest ½" (1.3 cm) below the beginning of the V-neck shaping. With smaller circ needle, with RS facing and beginning at bottom right edge of front opening, pickup and knit 278 (298, 318) sts evenly around neck opening as follows (using crochet hook for assistance, if desired): 76 (79, 84) sts along side of right front to beginning of V-neck shaping, 45 (51, 55) sts along right V-neck edge, 36 (38, 40) sts across back neck, 45 (51, 55) sts along left V-neck edge, 76 (79, 84) sts from V neck to lower edge of left front. Establish k2, p2 rib on next row (WS) as follows: P2, k2; repeat from * to last 2 sts, end p2. Work 1 row in rib as established. On the next row (WS), make five 2-row buttonholes as follows: *Work in rib pattern to marked buttonhole position, BO 2 sts; repeat from * 4 more times, work in rib pattern to end. On the next row (RS), CO 2 sts above each gap in the buttonhole row to complete buttonholes. Work 1 more row in rib. On the next row (RS), knit across all sts. BO all sts loosely as if to purl on next row. Weave in ends. Sew buttons to right front to correspond to buttonholes.

Jack's Aran Pullover—Adult

This pullover is perfect for the Young Men's/Active Casual guy or weekend woodsman. Featuring classic cables with contemporary fit and styling, it is sure to be a longtime favorite. Shown in a bulky blend of wool, alpaca, and acrylic, this outdoorsy pullover is soft and warm, perfect for winter weather. It's a good choice for the following fit issues: *Athletic and Average physiques, Long Neck, and the Tall or Thin guy.*

SPECIFICATIONS

Finished Sizes	Yarn	Needles	Notions	Gauge
Adult S (M, L, XL). 43½ (46, 48½, 54)" (110.5 [117, 123, 137] cm) finished chest. 24 (25, 26, 27)" (61 [63.5, 66, 68.5] cm) finished length. Sweater shown in size M.	Rowan Polar (60% wool, 30% alpaca, 10% acrylic; 109 yds [100 m]/100 g): #640 stony, 10 (11, 12, 13) skeins.	Size 11 (8 mm): straight or 29" (70-cm) circular (circ). Size 9 (5.5 mm): straight or 29" (70-cm) circ, 16" (40-cm) circ or double pointed (dpn). Adjust needle size if necessary to obtain the correct gauge.	Stitch markers; stitch holders; darning needle; cable needle (cn); scissors; measuring tape; crochet hook I (5.5 mm) for picking up stitches (optional).	Using larger needles, 12 sts and 20 rows = 4" (10 cm) in seed stitch (seed st); 40 sts lattice and cable pattern from chart measure approximately 9" (23 cm) wide; 8 sts of sleeve cable from chart measure approximately 2" (5 cm) wide. Check your gauge before you begin.

Seed Stitch (seed st)

Row 1: *K1, p1; repeat from *, ending k1 if there is an odd number of sts.

Row 2 and all following rows: Purl the knit sts, and knit the purl sts as they appear.

Back

With smaller needles, CO 70 (74, 78, 86) sts. Work in Stockinette stitch (St st) for 6 rows, or desired length of rolled edge, ending with a WS row, and increasing 8 sts evenly in last row—78 (82, 86, 94) sts. On the next row (RS), change to k2, p2 rib, and work as follows: *K2, p2; repeat from * to last 2 sts, end k2. On the following rows of k2, p2 rib, work all sts as they appear. Work in rib pattern for 2" (5 cm), ending with a RS row. Change to larger needles. On the next row (WS), work set-up row as follows, placing markers (pm) between st panels where indicated, if desired: Work 19

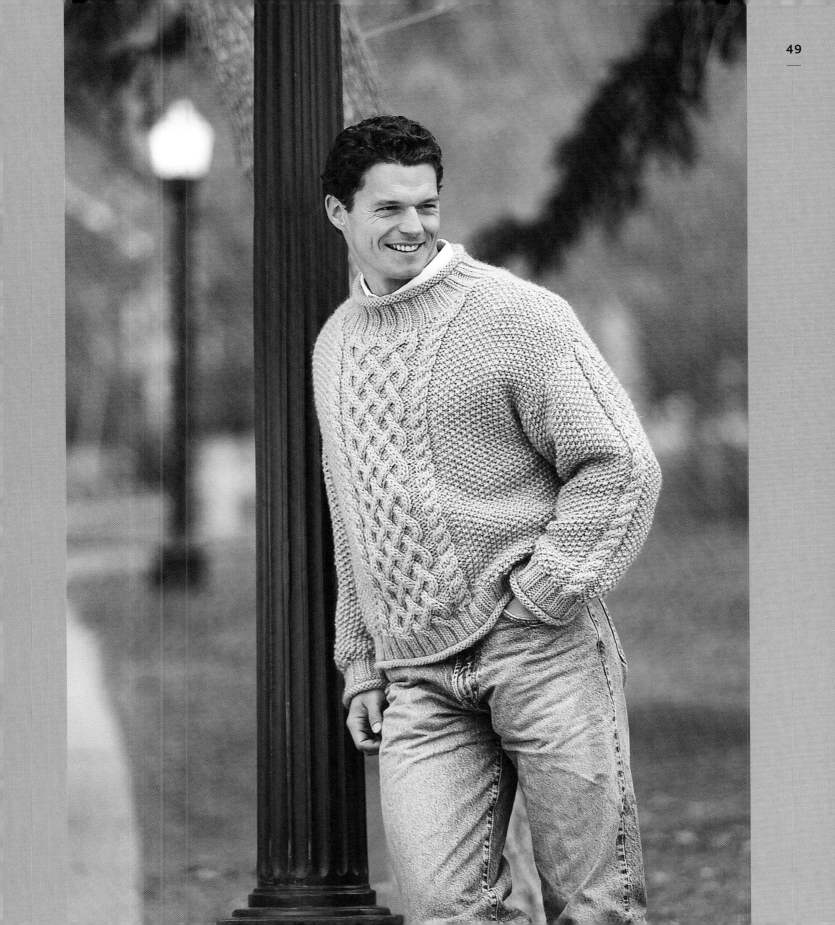

(21, 23, 27) sts seed st, pm, k2, p4, (k4, p4) 4 times, p2, pm, work 19 (21, 23, 27) sts seed st. On the next row (RS), work 19 (21, 23, 27) sts seed st, work center 40 sts from Row 1 of lattice and cable chart, work 19 (21, 23, 27) sts seed st. Work even in patterns as established until piece measures 13½ (14, 14½, 15)" (34.5 [35.5, 37, 38] cm) with bottom edge rolled up, ending with a WS row. Armhole shaping: BO 2 sts at beg of next 2 rows—74 (78, 82, 90) sts. Work even in patterns until piece measures 23½ (24½, 25½, 26½)" (59.5 [62, 65, 67.5] cm) with bottom edge rolled up, or ½" (1.3 cm) less than desired length, ending with a WS row. Shape back neck: Work 17 (19, 21, 25) sts in pattern, join new ball of yarn, BO center 40 sts, work in pattern to end. Working each side separately, work even in pattern until piece measures 24 (25, 26, 27)" (61 [63.5, 66, 68.5] cm) with bottom edge rolled up. Place 17 (19, 21, 25) sts for each shoulder on separate holders.

Front

Work as for back until piece measures 20½ (21½, 22½, 23½)" (52 [54.5, 57, 59.5] cm) with bottom edge rolled up, or 3½" (9 cm) less than desired length, ending with a WS row. Shape front neck: Work 25 (27, 29, 33) sts in pattern, join new ball of yarn, BO center 24 sts (lattice section of center panel), work in pattern to end. Working each side separately, decrease 1 st at each neck edge every other row 8 times—17 (19, 21, 25) sts at each side. Work even in pattern until piece measures 24 (25, 26, 27)" (61 [63.5, 66, 68.5] cm) with bottom edge rolled up. Place 17 (19, 21, 25) sts for each shoulder on separate holders.

Sleeves

Matching right front and back shoulders, with right sides of fabric held together, join right shoulder using three-needle bind-off technique. Repeat for left shoulder. With RS facing, using larger needles, beginning at inner corner of armhole notch, pick up and knit 66 (68, 72, 74) sts evenly from one armhole notch to the other (using crochet hook for assistance, if desired). On the next row (WS), work as follows, pm between st panels where indicated, if desired: Work 29 (30, 32, 33) sts seed st, pm, k2, p4, k2, pm, work 29 (30, 32, 33) sts seed st. On the

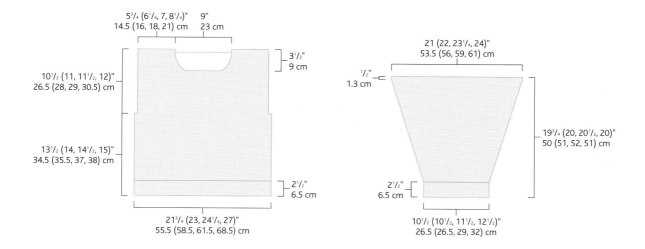

next row (RS), work as follows: 29 (30, 32, 33) sts seed st, 8 sts from Row 1 of sleeve cable chart, 29 (30, 32, 33) sts seed st. Shape sleeve: Continue in patterns, and beginning with the next RS row, decrease 1 st at each side every 6 rows 8 (7, 6, 7) times, then every 4 rows 8 (10, 12, 10) times—34 (34, 36, 40) sts. Work even until piece measures 17¼ (17½, 18, 17½)" (43 [44.5, 45.5, 44.5] cm) from pickup row, or 2½" (6.5 cm) less than desired length, ending with a WS row, and decreasing 0 (0, 2, 2) sts evenly across in last row—34 (34, 34, 38) sts. Change to smaller needles. Work in k2, p2 rib as for back for 2" (5 cm), ending with a WS row. On the next row (RS), knit across all sts. Work even in St st for 6 rows. BO all sts loosely.

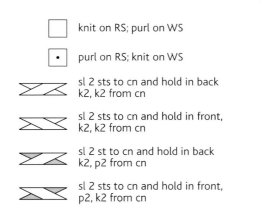

knit on RS; purl on WS

purl on RS; knit on WS

sl 2 sts to cn and hold in back
k2, k2 from cn

sl 2 sts to cn and hold in front,
k2, k2 from cn

sl 2 st to cn and hold in back
k2, p2 from cn

sl 2 sts to cn and hold in front,
p2, k2 from cn

Finishing

Lightly steam block only if needed; blocking can compromise the rich texture of the knitting you have worked so hard to achieve. Sew sleeve and side seams, reversing the seam for the rolled edges so RS of seam will show when purl side of St st sections rolls to the outside of garment. Weave in ends.

Neckband

With smaller 16" (40-cm) circ needle, with RS facing and beginning at left shoulder seam, pickup and knit 80 sts evenly around neck opening as follows (using crochet hook for assistance, if desired): 12 sts along side of left front neck, 20 sts across center front, 12 sts along side of right front neck, 36 sts across back neck. Join for working in the round (rnd), and pm to indicate beginning of rnd. Work k2, p2 rib in the rnd for 2½" (6.5 cm), or ½" (1.3 cm) less than desired length for neckband. Change to St st and knit 6 rnds. BO all sts loosely as if to knit on next rnd. Weave in ends.

Lattice and Cable

| | | | | | | | | | | | | | | | | | | | | | | | | | | 8 |
| | | | | | | | | | | | | | | | | | | | | | | | | | | 7 |

6
5
4
3
2
1

Sleeve Cable

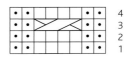

4
3
2
1

Jack's Aran Pullover—Child

The junior version of Jack's Aran Pullover is sure to be a favorite with your little guy. The fit is roomy and the yarn is soft and warm. The pullover is versatile enough for dressy or casual occasions, and it can be worn alone in place of a fleece pullover or jacket.

SPECIFICATIONS

Finished Sizes	Yarn	Needles	Notions	Gauge
Child S (M, L), to fit 4 (6/8, 10/12) years. 32½ (35½, 38)" (82.5 [90, 96.5] cm) finished chest. 17 (19, 20)" (43 [48.5, 51] cm) finished length. Sweater shown in size M, to fit 6/8 years.	Rowan Polar (60% wool, 30% alpaca, 10% acrylic; 109 yds [100 m]/100 g): #641 red hot, 5 (6, 7) skeins.	Size 11 (8 mm): straight. Size 9 (5.5 mm): straight, and 16" (40-cm) circ or double pointed (dpn). Adjust needle size if necessary to obtain the correct gauge.	Stitch markers; stitch holders; darning needle; cable needle (cn); scissors; measuring tape; crochet hook I (5.5 mm) for picking up stitches (optional).	Using larger needles, 12 sts and 20 rows = 4" (10 cm) in seed stitch (seed st); 40 sts lattice and cable pattern from chart measure approximately 9" (23 cm) wide; 8 sts of sleeve cable from chart measure approximately 2" (5 cm) wide. Check your gauge before you begin.

Seed Stitch (seed st)

Row 1: *K1, p1; repeat from *, ending k1 if there is an odd number of sts.

Row 2 and all following rows: Purl the knit sts, and knit the purl sts as they appear.

Back

With smaller needles, CO 54 (58, 62) sts. Work in Stockinette stitch (St st) for 6 rows, or desired length of rolled edge, ending with a WS row, and increasing 8 sts evenly in last row—62 (66, 70) sts. On the next row (RS), change to k2, p2 rib, and work as follows: *K2, p2; repeat from * to last 2 sts, end k2. On the following rows of k2, p2 rib, work all sts as they appear. Work in rib pattern for 7 rows, ending with a RS row. Change to larger needles. On the next row (WS), work set-up row as follows, placing markers (pm) between st panels where indicated, if desired: Work 11 (13, 15) sts seed st, pm, k2, p4, (k4, p4) 4 times, p2, pm, work 11 (13, 15) sts seed st. On the next row (RS), work 11

(13, 15) sts seed st, work center 40 sts from Row 1 of lattice and cable chart, work 11 (13, 15) sts seed st. Work even in patterns as established until piece measures 8¾ (9½, 10)" (22 [24, 25.5] cm) with bottom edge rolled up, ending with a WS row. Armhole shaping: BO 2 sts at beg of next 2 rows—58 (62, 66) sts. Work even in patterns until piece measures 16½ (18½, 19½)" (42 [47, 49.5] cm) with bottom edge rolled up, or ½" (1.3 cm) less than desired length, ending with a WS row. Shape back neck: Work 11 (13, 15) sts in patterns, join new ball of yarn, BO center 36 sts, work in patterns to end. Working each side separately, work even in patterns until piece measures 17 (19, 20)" (43 [48.5, 51] cm) with bottom edge rolled up. Place 11 (13, 15) sts for each shoulder on separate holders.

Front

Work as for back until piece measures 13½ (15½, 16½)" (34.5 [39.5, 42] cm with bottom edge rolled up, or 3½" (9 cm) less than desired length, ending with a WS row. Shape front neck: Work 19 (21, 23) sts in patterns, join new ball of yarn, BO center 20 sts, work in patterns to end. Working each side separately, decrease 1 st at each neck edge every other row 8 times—11 (13, 15) sts at each

side. Work even in patterns until piece measures 17 (19, 20)" (43 [48.5, 51] cm) with bottom edge rolled up. Place 11 (13, 15) sts for each shoulder on separate holders.

Sleeves

Matching right front and back shoulders, with right sides of fabric held together, join right shoulder using three-needle bind-off technique. Repeat for left shoulder. With RS facing, using larger needles, beginning at inner corner of armhole notch, pick up and knit 52 (60, 62) sts evenly from one armhole notch to the other (using crochet hook for assistance, if desired). On the next row (WS), work as follows, pm between st panels where indicated, if desired: Work 22 (26, 27) sts seed st, pm, k2, p4, k2, pm, work 22 (26, 27) sts seed st. On the next row (RS), work as follows: 22 (26, 27) sts seed st, 8 sts from Row 1 of sleeve cable chart, 22 (26, 27) sts seed st. Shape sleeve: Continue in patterns, and beginning with the next RS row, decrease 1 st at each side every 4 rows 8 (6, 10) times, then every other row 5 (11, 6) times—26 (26, 30) sts. Work even until piece measures 9½ (10½, 11½)" (24 [26.5, 29] cm) from pickup row, or 1½" (3.8 cm) less than desired length, ending with a WS row. Change to smaller needles. Work in k2,

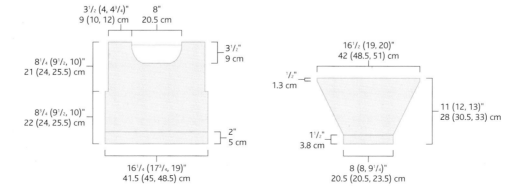

p2 rib as for back for 6 rows, ending with a WS row. On the next row (RS), knit across all sts. Work even in St st for 6 rows. BO all sts loosely.

Finishing

Lightly steam block only if needed; blocking can compromise the rich texture of the knitting you have worked so hard to achieve. Sew sleeve and side seams, reversing the seam for the rolled edges so RS of seam will show when purl side of St st sections rolls to the outside of garment. Weave in ends.

Neckband

With smaller 16" (40-cm) circ or dpn, with RS facing and beginning at left shoulder seam, pickup and knit 76 sts evenly around neck opening as follows (using crochet hook for assistance, if desired): 12 sts along side of left front neck, 20 sts across center front, 12 sts along side of right front neck, 32 sts across back neck. Join for working in the round (rnd), and pm to indicate beginning of rnd. Work k2, p2 rib in the rnd for 2" (5 cm), or ½" (1.3 cm) less than desired length for neckband. Change to St st and knit 6 rnds. BO all sts loosely as if to knit on next rnd. Weave in ends.

 knit on RS; purl on WS

 purl on RS; knit on WS

 sl 2 sts to cn and hold in back
k2, k2 from cn

 sl 2 sts to cn and hold in front,
k2, k2 from cn

 sl 2 st to cn and hold in back
k2, p2 from cn

 sl 2 sts to cn and hold in front,
p2, k2 from cn

Lattice and Cable

8
7
6
5
4
3
2
1

Sleeve Cable

4
3
2
1

Hyland Argyle Vest

THE ARGYLE INTARSIA PATTERN featured in this smart set of vests has its roots in the Scottish highlands. The vest's name pays homage to my family, the Hyland Clan, which originally hailed from Ireland but more recently called Bay Ridge, Brooklyn, home! A very dapper garment for the young or young at heart, this duo is knitted in a rich silk/alpaca blend that creates a lightweight, drapey fabric with a touch of sheen. The Hyland design is perfect for any style type and every occasion, be it a day at the office, school pictures, or a semi-formal gathering. These vests are easy to knit, worked in the round to the underarm. The simple color blocks are a good introduction for the knitter new to intarsia. To keep things simple, the argyle's contrasting crossing lines can be added at a later time using duplicate stitch.

Hyland Argyle Vest—Adult

An updated classic, this vest features a refined argyle motif at the chest, a hemmed lower edge, and a trim fit. Depending on the wearer's attitude and the rest of his outfit, the vest is versatile enough for sophisticated casual or very dressy. Knitted in the round to the underarm and joined at the shoulder with a three-needle bind-off, it has no seams to sew, and finishing is a breeze. This handsome garment is perfect for the Young Professional/ Modern Casual or Corporate/Traditional guy. It's a good choice for the following fit issues: *Rounded Shoulders, Tall and Athletic physiques.*

SPECIFICATIONS

Finished Sizes	Yarn	Needles	Notions	Gauge
Adult S (M, L, XL). 40 (43, 48, 52)" (101.5 [109, 122, 132] cm) finished chest. 25 (26, 27, 28)" (63.5 [66, 68.5, 71] cm) finished length. Vest shown in size M.	Cascade Success (50% alpaca, 50% silk; 123 yds [112 m]/50 g): #609 silver (MC), 8 (9, 10, 12) skeins; #606 black (C1) and #607 white (C2), 1 skein each.	Size 4 (3.5 mm): straight and 29" (70-cm) circular (circ). Size 2 (2.5 mm): 16" (40-cm) circ or double pointed (dpn). Adjust needle size if necessary to obtain the correct gauge.	Stitch markers; stitch holders; darning needle; scissors; measuring tape; crochet hook B (2.5 mm) for picking up stitches (optional).	Using larger needles, 24 sts and 32 rows = 4" (10 cm) in Stockinette stitch (St st). Check your gauge before you begin.

Body

With larger 29" (70-cm) circ needle and MC, CO 236 (254, 284, 308) sts. Join, being careful not to twist, and place marker (pm) to indicate beginning of round (rnd). Work 9 rnds even in St st (knit all sts every rnd). In next rnd, increase 4 sts evenly—240 (258, 288, 312) sts. Purl one rnd for fold line. Work even until piece measures 1¼" (3.2 cm) from purled fold line. Change to C2 and knit 1 rnd. Change back to MC and work even until piece measures 14 (14½, 15½, 16)" (35.5 [37, 39.5, 40.5] cm) from purled fold line, or desired length to armholes. On the next rnd, divide for front and back as follows: K103 (109, 119, 131) sts, BO 17 (20, 25, 25) sts, k103 (109, 119, 131) sts, BO 17 (20, 25, 25) sts. The group of sts to be worked next are the sts for the front.

Front

Leaving sts for back unworked on the cable part of the circ needle, work front sts back and forth in rows. Shape armhole: Beginning with the first row (RS), decrease 1

st at each end every other row 8 (8, 10, 10) times—87 (93, 99, 111) sts, ending with a WS row—front measures approximately 2 (2, 2½, 2½)" (5 [5, 6.5, 6.5] cm) from dividing rnd. For size S and M *only,* work even in St st until piece measures 2½" (6.5 cm) from dividing rnd, ending with a WS row. For all sizes, on the next row (RS) join C1 and C2 as needed, and work argyle pattern from chart over 87 (93, 99, 111) sts, beginning and ending as indicated for your size. If desired, work only the C1 diamonds now, and add the C2 diagonal lines later using duplicate stitch. When Row 13 of argyle chart has been completed, front measures approximately 4" (10 cm) from dividing rnd. Shape V neck: (WS) P43 (46, 49, 55) sts, place center st on holder, join second ball of yarn, p43 (46, 49, 55) sts to end. Working each side separately, decrease 1 st at neck edge every 3 rows 5 (4, 4, 6) times, then every other row 16 (19, 19, 19) times—22 (23, 26, 30) sts. Work even until piece measures 25 (26, 27, 28)" (63.5 [66, 68.5, 71] cm) from purled fold line, or desired length. Place 22 (23, 26, 30) sts for each shoulder on separate holders.

Back

Join MC to sts on cable needle for back with RS facing—103 (109, 119, 131) sts. Work as for front through completion of the argyle chart—87 (93, 99, 111) sts. With MC only, work even until piece measures ½" (1.3 cm) less than front, ending with a WS row. Shape back neck: Knit 22 (23, 26, 30) sts, join second ball of yarn, BO center 43 (47, 47, 51) sts, knit to end. Working each side separately, work even until piece measures 25 (26, 27, 28)" (63.5 [66, 68.5, 71] cm) from purled fold line, or same length as front. Place 22 (23, 26, 30) sts for each shoulder on separate holders.

Finishing

Matching right front and back shoulders, with right sides of fabric held together, join right shoulder using three-needle bind-off technique. Repeat for left shoulder. Fold bottom hem to WS along purled turning rnd and slip-stitch into place. Lightly steam block only if needed. Weave in ends.

V-neck Band

Using MC, with RS facing and smaller circ needle, beginning at left shoulder seam, pick up and knit 151 (156, 156, 165) sts around neck opening as follows (using crochet hook for assistance, if desired): 50 (52, 52, 54) sts along left side neck, pm, knit 1 st from center front holder, pick up and knit 50 (52, 52, 54) sts along right side neck, pick up and knit 50 (51, 51, 56) sts across back neck. Next rnd: Work in k1, p1 rib to 2 sts before first marker, ssk, slip marker (sl m), k1 (center st), sl m, k2tog, work in k1, p1

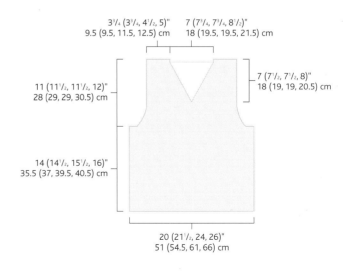

rib to end—149 (154, 154, 163) sts. Work 4 more rnds in this manner, decreasing on either side of center marked st on each rnd—141 (146, 146, 155) sts. Change to C2 and work 1 rnd, decreasing as before—139 (144, 144, 153) sts. Change to MC and knit 1 rnd, decreasing as before—137 (142, 142, 151) sts. With MC, work 3 rnds k1, p1 rib, decreasing as before—131 (136, 136, 145) sts. BO all sts loosely in rib pattern with MC. Weave in ends.

Armhole Bands

Using MC, with RS facing and smaller 16" (40-cm) circ or dpn, beginning at base of armhole pick up and knit 148 (158, 158, 168) sts evenly around armhole edge, (using crochet hook for assistance, if desired). Join for working in the rnd, and work 6 rnds k1, p1 rib. BO all sts loosely in rib pattern. Weave in ends. Repeat for other armhole.

Argyle Chart—Adult

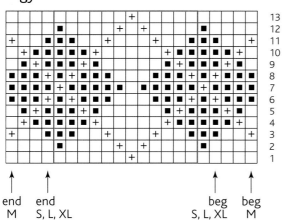

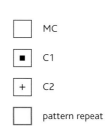

□ MC

■ C1

+ C2

□ pattern repeat

Hyland Argyle Vest—Child

ॐ

This vest features a dressy, classic style, with roomy sizing for a very modern (and growing) boy. The alpaca and silk blend creates a lightweight but warm fabric with incredible drape. For formal occasions, this vest can substitute for a suit, and your young man will appreciate the switch.

SPECIFICATIONS

Finished Sizes	Yarn	Needles	Notions	Gauge
Child S (M, L), to fit 4 (6/8, 10/12) years. 32 (34, 38)" (81.5 [86.5, 96.5] cm) finished chest. 17 (18½, 20)" (43 [47, 51] cm) finished length. Vest shown in size S, to fit 4 years.	Cascade Success (50% alpaca, 50% silk; 123 yds [112 m]/50 g): #608 dark blue (MC), 5 (6, 7) skeins; #671 light blue (C1) and #607 white (C2), 1 skein each.	Size 4 (3.5 mm): 29" (70-cm) circular (circ). Size 2 (2.5 mm): 16" (40 cm) circ or double pointed (dpn). Adjust needle size if necessary to obtain the correct gauge.	Stitch markers; stitch holders; darning needle; scissors; measuring tape; crochet hook B (2.5 mm) for picking up stitches (optional).	Using larger needles, 24 sts and 32 rows = 4" (10 cm) in Stockinette stitch (St st). Check your gauge before you begin.

Body

With larger circ needle and MC, CO 190 (202, 226) sts. Join, being careful not to twist, and place marker (pm) to indicate beginning of round (rnd). Work 9 rnds even in St st (knit all sts every rnd). In next rnd, increase 4 sts evenly—194 (206, 230) sts. Purl one rnd for fold line. Work even until piece measures 1¼" (3.2 cm) from purled fold line. Change to C2 and knit 1 rnd. Change back to MC and work even until piece measures 8½ (9¼, 10)" (21.5 [23.5, 25.5] cm) from purled fold line, or desired length to armholes. On the next rnd, divide for front and back as follows: K81 (87, 97) sts, BO 16 (16, 18) sts, k81 (87, 97) sts, BO 16 (16, 18) sts. The group of sts to be worked next are the sts for the front.

Front

Leaving sts for back unworked on the cable part of the circ needle, work front sts back and forth in rows. Shape armhole: Beginning with the first row (RS), dec 1 st at each end every other row 8 (8, 9) times—65 (71, 79) sts, ending with a WS row—front measures approximately 2 (2, 2¼)" (5 [5, 5.5] cm) from dividing rnd. On the next row (RS) join C1 and C2 as needed, and work argyle pattern from chart over 65 (71, 79) sts, beginning and ending as indicated for your size. If desired, work only the C1 diamonds now, and add the C2 diagonal lines later using duplicate stitch. When Row 13 of argyle chart has been completed, front measures approximately 3¾ (3¾, 4)" (9.5 [9.5, 10] cm) from

dividing rnd. Shape V neck: (WS) P32 (35, 39) sts, place center st on holder, join second ball of yarn, p32 (35, 39) sts to end. Working each side separately, decrease 1 st at neck edge every other row 18 (12, 11) times, then every 3 rows 0 (6, 8) times—14 (17, 20) sts. Work even until piece measures 17 (18½, 20)" (43 [47, 51] cm) from purled fold line, or desired length. Place 14 (17, 20) sts for each shoulder on separate holders.

Back

Join MC to sts on cable needle for back with RS facing—81 (87, 97) sts. Work as for front through completion of the armhole shaping and argyle chart—65 (71, 79) sts. With MC only, work even until piece measures ¼" (0.6 cm) less than front, ending with a WS row. Shape back neck: Knit 14 (17, 20) sts, join second ball of yarn, BO center 37 (37, 39) sts, knit to end. Working each side separately, work even until piece measures 17 (18½, 20") (43 [47, 51] cm) from purled fold line, or same length as front. Place 14 (17, 20) sts for each shoulder on separate holders.

Finishing

Matching right front and back shoulders, with right sides of fabric held together, join right shoulder using three-needle bind-off technique. Repeat for left shoulder. Fold bottom hem to WS along purled turning rnd and slip-stitch into place. Lightly steam block only if needed. Weave in ends.

V-neck Band

Using MC and smaller circ needle, with RS facing, beginning at left shoulder seam, pick up and knit 117 (129, 139) sts around neck opening as follows (using crochet hook for assistance, if desired): 39 (45, 49) sts along left side neck, pm, knit 1 st from center front holder, pm, pick up and knit 39 (45, 49) sts along right side neck, pick up and knit 38 (38, 40) sts across back neck. Join for working in the rnd and place marker to indicate beginning of rnd. Next rnd: Work in k1, p1 rib to 2 sts before first marker, ssk, slip marker (sl m), k1 (center st), sl m, k2tog, work in k1, p1 rib to end—115 (127, 137) sts. Work 7 more rnds in this manner, decreasing on either side of center marked st on each rnd—101 (113, 123) sts. BO all sts loosely in rib. Weave in ends.

Armhole Bands

Using MC, with RS facing and smaller 16" (40-cm) circ or dpn, beginning at base of armhole pick up and knit 108 (116, 126) sts evenly around armhole edge, (using crochet hook for assistance, if desired). Join for working in the rnd, and work 6 rnds k1, p1 rib. BO all sts loosely in rib pattern. Weave in ends. Repeat for other armhole.

Argyle Chart—Child

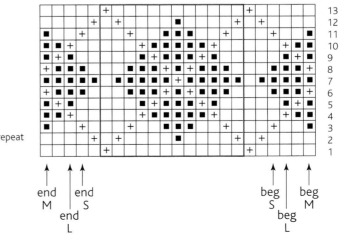

2¼ (2¾, 3¼)"
5.5 (7, 8.5) cm

6¼ (6¼, 6½)"
16 (16, 16.5) cm

4¾ (5½, 6)"
12 (14, 15) cm

8½ (9¼, 10)"
21.5 (23.5, 25.5) cm

8½ (9¼, 10)"
21.5 (23.5, 25.5) cm

16 (17, 19)"
40.5 (43, 48.5) cm

MC

■ C1

+ C2

pattern repeat

Garter Stitch Aran

THE GARTER STITCH ARAN COLLECTION features classic Aran design elements, unified by the use of garter stitch at the waistband, side panels, and as fill stitch in the diamond motif. The pullover features a soft washable wool for an updated casual feel. My husband's favorite in the collection, its warm coffee color has earned it the nickname of the "latte" sweater. The cardigan features a rich red and classic V-neck style for a slightly more traditional, dressy feel. A comfortable fit is ensured in all versions by slightly loose and straight edges of the garter stitch bands at the waist and cuffs.

Garter Stitch Aran Cardigan, with Gloves

ॐ

Like its companion sweater—the Garter Stitch Aran Pullover—the Garter Stitch Aran Cardigan combines casual elements with modern style. Knitted in a rich tone and thick wool, this V-neck cardigan easily dresses up or down. It's trimmed with garter stitch in place of traditional ribbing, making it great for all style types. Choose it for the following fit issues: *All physiques, Short, Rounded Shoulders, Thin.* The coordinating gloves are a perfect complement to any of the Garter Stitch Aran projects.

SPECIFICATIONS

Finished Sizes	Yarn	Needles	Notions	Gauge
Adult S (M, L, XL). 42 (47, 50, 54)" (106.5 [119.5, 127, 137] cm) finished chest. 24½ (25½, 26½, 27½)" (62 [65, 67.5, 70] cm) finished length. Sweater shown in size M. Gloves approximately 8½" (21.5 cm) around, measured at base of fingers.	Ashford/Crystal Palace Tekapo (100% wool; 218 yds [199 m]/100 g): #09 dark red, 8 (9, 10, 11) skeins for cardigan; 1 skein for gloves.	Size 8 (5 mm): straight. Size 7 (4.5 mm): straight and 16" (40-cm) circ. For gloves only, size 5 (3.75 mm): set of 4 double pointed (dpn). Adjust needle size if necessary to obtain the correct gauge.	Stitch markers; stitch holders; darning needle; cable needle (cn); scissors; measuring tape; five ¾" (2-cm) buttons (shown: One World Button Supply, NPL 238-20BT Burnt Horn Rough Tablet 20 mm); crochet hook H (5 mm) for picking up stitches (optional).	Using larger needles, 19 sts and 28 rows = 4" (10 cm) in garter stitch (knit all sts every row). 12-st cable panels measure 1⅞" (4.8 cm) wide; 25-st center diamond panel measures 4½" (11.5 cm) wide. Using dpn needles for gloves, 24 sts and 32 rows = 4"(10 cm) in Stockinette stitch (St st). Check your gauge before you begin.

Back

With smaller needles, CO 114 (125, 133, 143) sts. Work in garter st for 9 rows. Change to larger needles. On the next row (WS), set up patterns as follows, increasing sts and placing markers (pm) between each st panel where indicated:

K1 (4, 8, 8) garter st(s), pm;

K1, p1, k2, p2, M1, p1, k2, p1, k1 (left cable), pm;

K4 (5, 5, 7) garter st, pm;

K1, p1, k8, p2, M1, p2, k8, p1, k1 (center diamond), pm;

K4 (5, 5, 7) garter st, pm;

K1, p1, k2, p2, M1, p1, k2, p1, k1 (left cable), pm;

K4 (5, 5, 7) garter st, pm;

K1, p1, k2, p2, M1, p1, k2, p1, k1 (right cable), pm;

K4 (5, 5, 7) garter st, pm;

K1, p1, k8, p2, M1, p2, k8, p1, k1 (center diamond), pm;

K4 (5, 5, 7) garter st, pm;

K1, p1, k2, p2, M1, p1, k2, p1, k1 (right cable), pm;

K1 (4, 8, 8) garter st(s)—120 (131, 139, 149) sts.

On the next row (RS), work in garter st or Row 1 from each chart as follows: 1 (4, 8, 8) st(s) garter st, 12 sts right cable, 4 (5, 5, 7) sts garter st, 25 sts center diamond, 4 (5, 5, 7) sts garter st, 12 sts right cable, 4 (5, 5, 7) sts garter st, 12 sts left cable, 4 (5, 5, 7) sts garter st, 25 sts center diamond, 4 (5, 5, 7) sts garter st, 12 sts left cable, 1 (4, 8, 8) st(s) garter st. Work even in patterns as established until piece measures 14½ (15, 15½, 16)" (37 [38, 39.5, 40.5] cm) from beginning, ending with a WS row. Armhole shaping: BO 2 sts at beg of next 2 rows—116 (127, 135, 145) sts. Work even in pattern until piece measures 23½ (24½, 25½, 26½)" (59.5 [62, 65, 67.5] cm) from beginning, ending with a WS row. Shape back neck: Work 37 (41, 43, 46) sts in pattern, join new ball of yarn, BO center 42 (45, 49, 53) sts, work in pattern to end. Working each side separately, work even in pattern until piece measures 24½ (25½, 26½, 27½)" (62 [65, 67.5, 70] cm) from beginning. Place 37 (41, 43, 46) sts for each shoulder on separate holders.

Right Front

With smaller needles, CO 60 (66, 70, 76) sts. Work in garter st for 9 rows. Change to larger needles. On the next row (WS), set up patterns as follows, increasing sts and placing markers (pm) between each st panel where indicated:

K1 (4, 8, 8) garter st(s), pm;

K1, p1, k2, p2, M1, p1, k2, p1, k1 (left cable), pm;

K4 (5, 5, 7) garter st, pm;

K1, p1, k8, p2, M1, p2, k8, p1, k1 (center diamond), pm;

K4 (5, 5, 7) garter st, pm;

K1, p1, k2, p2, M1, p1, k2, p1, k1 (left cable), pm;

K5 (6, 6, 8) garter st for front band—63 (69, 73, 79) sts.

On the next row (RS), work in garter st or Row 1 from each chart as follows: 5 (6, 6, 8) sts garter st for front band, 12 sts left cable, 4 (5, 5, 7) sts garter st, 25 sts center diamond, 4 (5, 5, 7) sts garter st, 12 sts left cable, 1 (4, 8, 8) st(s) garter st. Work even in patterns as established until piece measures 14½ (15, 15½, 16)" (37 [38, 39.5, 40.5] cm) from beginning, ending with a RS row. Armhole shaping: BO 2 sts at beg of next WS row—61 (67, 71, 77) sts. On the next row (RS) begin V-neck shaping as follows: K5 (6, 6, 8) sts for garter st front band, remove existing marker, p1 (first st of left cable), place new marker, ssk, work in pattern to end—1 st decreased. Work 1 row even. Repeat the last 2 rows 18 (19, 21, 22) more times, decreasing by working ssk after the front band marker on each RS row—42 (47, 49, 54) sts. *Note:* When there are not enough sts in the first left cable panel to work the cable crossings, work these sts in St st until they are decreased away. Work even until piece measures 24½ (25½, 26½, 27½)" (62 [65, 67.5, 70] cm) from beginning, ending with a WS row. Work first 5 (6, 6, 8) sts for garter st front band, place remaining 37 (41, 43, 46) sts on holder for shoulder. Working back and forth on front band sts only, work in garter st until front band extension measures 3¾ (4, 4½, 4¾)" (9.5 [10, 11.5, 12] cm) when slightly stretched, or halfway across back neck. BO front band sts loosely.

Left Front

The left front is worked as for right front, reversing the cables, and making two-row buttonholes in front band as given below. With smaller needles, CO 60 (66, 70, 76) sts. Work in garter st for 6 rows. On the next row (RS), knit to last 4 (4, 4, 5) sts, BO 2 sts, knit to end. On the following row (WS), CO 2 sts above gap in previous row to complete buttonhole. Knit 1 more row. Change to larger needles. On the next row (WS), set up patterns as follows, increasing sts and placing markers (pm) between each st panel where indicated:

K5 (6, 6, 8) garter st for front band

K1, p1, k2, p2, M1, p1, k2, p1, k1 (right cable), pm;

K4 (5, 5, 7) garter st, pm;

K1, p1, k8, p2, M1, p2, k8, p1, k1 (center diamond), pm;

K4 (5, 5, 7) garter st, pm;

K1, p1, k2, p2, M1, p1, k2, p1, k1 (right cable), pm;

K1 (4, 8, 8) garter st(s)—63 (69, 73, 79) sts.

On the next row (RS), work in garter st or Row 1 from each chart as follows: 1 (4, 8, 8) st(s) garter st, 12 sts right cable, 4 (5, 5, 7) sts garter st, 25 sts center diamond, 4 (5, 5, 7) sts garter st, 12 sts right cable, 5 (6, 6, 8) sts garter st for front band. Mark positions for five evenly spaced buttons on right front, the lowest button corresponding to the buttonhole already worked in lower band of left front, and the highest ½" (1.3 cm) below beginning of V-neck shaping. Work even in patterns as established, working a 2-st, 2-row buttonhole as before to correspond with each marked button position on right front, until piece measures 14½ (15, 15½, 16)" (37 [38, 39.5, 40.5] cm) from beginning, ending with a WS row. Armhole shaping: BO 2 sts at beg of next RS row, work to end—61 (67, 71, 77) sts. Work 1 WS row even. On the next row (RS) begin V-neck shaping as follows: Work to last 8 (9, 9, 11) sts, k2tog, remove existing marker, p1 (last st of right cable panel), place new marker, k5 (6, 6, 8) garter st for front band—1 st decreased. Work 1 row even. Repeat the last 2 rows 18 (19, 21, 22) more times, decreasing by working k2tog on the 2 sts before the front band marker on each RS row—42 (47, 49, 54) sts. *Note:* When there are not enough sts in the last right cable panel to work the cable crossings, work these sts in St st until they are decreased away. Work even until piece measures 24½ (25½, 26½, 27½)" (62 [65, 67.5, 70] cm) from beginning, ending with a RS row. Work first 5 (6, 6, 8) sts for garter st front band, place 37 (41, 43, 46) sts on holder for shoulder. Working back and forth on front band sts only, work in garter st until front band extension measures 3¾ (4, 4½, 4¾)" (9.5 [10, 11.5, 12] cm) when slightly stretched, or halfway across back neck. BO front band sts loosely.

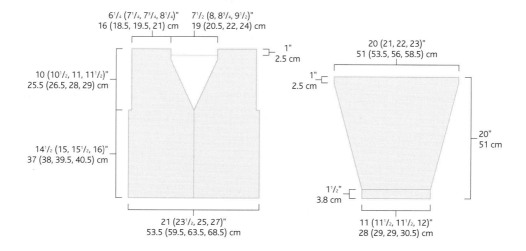

Sleeves

Matching right front and back shoulders, with right sides of fabric held together, join right shoulder using three-needle bind-off technique. Repeat for left shoulder. With RS facing, using larger needles, beginning at inner corner of armhole notch, pick up and knit 102 (106, 110, 116) sts evenly from one armhole notch to the other (using crochet hook for assistance, if desired). On the next row (WS), set up patterns as follows, increasing and placing markers between each st panel where indicated:

K31 (33, 35, 38) garter st, pm;

K1, p1, k2, p2, M1, p1, k2, p1, k1 (left cable), pm;

K1, p2, k6, M1, k6, p2, k1 (center diamond), pm;

K1, p1, k2, p2, M1, p1, k2, p1, k1 (right cable), pm;

K31 (33, 35, 38) garter st—105 (109, 113, 119) sts.

On the next row (RS), work in garter st or indicated row from each chart as follows: 31 (33, 35, 38) sts garter st, 12 sts right cable Row 1, 19 indicated center sts from center diamond chart Row 19, 12 sts left cable Row 1, 31 (33, 35, 38) garter st. Work even in patterns for 5 more rows—piece measures approximately 1" (2.5 cm) from edge of body. Shape sleeve: Beginning with the next row (RS), decrease 1 st at each side every 6 rows 14 (12, 8, 4) times, then every 4 rows 8 (11, 17, 23) times—61 (63, 63, 65) sts. Work even until piece measures 18½" (47 cm) from pickup row, or 1½" (3.8 cm) less than desired length, ending with a WS row. Change to smaller needles. On the next row (RS), knit across all sts, decreasing 11 sts evenly—50 (52, 52, 54) sts. Work even in garter st for 1½" (3.8 cm). BO all sts loosely as if to knit.

Finishing

Lightly steam block only if needed; blocking can com-

promise the rich texture of the Aran knitting you have worked so hard to achieve. Sew straight sections at top of sleeves to armhole notches. Sew sleeve and side seams, carefully matching garter st cuffs and bottom borders at sides. Sew BO edges of front band extensions together, and sew extension in place across back neck. Sew on buttons. Weave in ends.

Gloves

Both gloves are worked exactly the same, so they can be worn on either hand to increase their wearing life. To dress up the gloves, consider sewing on leather palm patches, or adding a basic rope cable up the back using the rope cable charts from the Classic Camel Vest (see page 76). An option for fingerless gloves is given at the end of the directions.

Cuff

CO 52 sts, and divide as evenly as possible over 3 needles. Join for working in the round (rnd), being careful not to twist, and place marker (pm) to indicate beginning of rnd. Work in k1, p1 rib for 4" (10 cm) or desired length for cuff. Knit 1 rnd.

Thumb Gusset

Begin thumb shaping as follows: K25, pm, make 1 st (M1), k2, M1, pm, knit to end—4 sts between markers, 54 sts total. Knit 1 rnd even. Increase rnd: Knit to first m, slip marker (sl m), M1, knit to second m, M1, sl m, knit to end. Repeat the last 2 rnds until there are 20 sts between markers for thumb gusset—70 sts total. Next rnd: Knit to first m, remove m, place next 20 sts for thumb on holder, remove second m, CO 2 sts in above the gap created by placing the thumb sts on hold, knit to end—52 sts.

Hand

Work even in St st until glove measures 4½" (11.5 cm) above the rib.

Little Finger

K6, place next 40 sts on holder, CO 1 st, knit remaining 6 sts of rnd—13 sts. Divide sts as evenly as possible on 3 needles and work in St st for 2¼" (5.5 cm). Dec Rnd 1: *K1, k2tog; rep from * to last st, end k1—9 sts. Work 1 rnd even. Dec Rnd 2: K2tog 4 times, k1—5 sts. Break

yarn, leaving 6" (15-cm) tail. Using a darning needle, draw tail through rem sts and pull snugly to close fingertip. Weave in ends.

Ring Finger

Transfer first 7 and last 6 sts from holder to 2 needles. Join yarn at base of little finger. Pick up and knit 1 st from CO st at base of little finger, k6, CO 1 st, k6 to end—15 sts. Divide sts on 3 needles and work in St st for 2½" (6.5 cm) or ½" (1.3 cm) less than desired length of finger. Dec Rnd 1: *K1, k2tog; rep from * to end—10 sts. Work 1 rnd even. Dec Rnd 2: K2tog around—5 sts. Finish as for little finger.

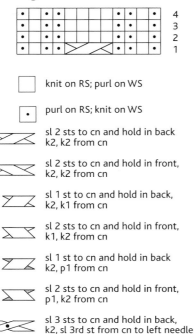

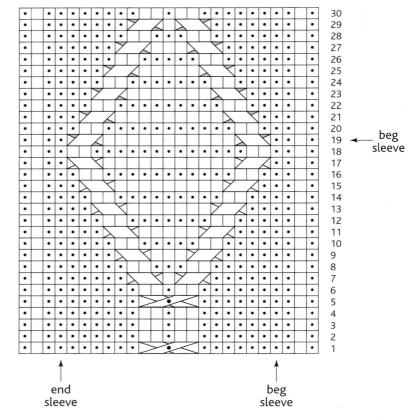

Middle Finger

Transfer first 6 and last 7 sts from holder to 2 needles. Join yarn at base of ring finger. Pick up and knit 1 st from CO st at base of ring finger, k6, CO 1 st, k7 to end—15 sts. Divide sts on 3 needles and work in St st for 2¾" (7 cm) or ½" (1.3 cm) less than desired length of finger. Work decrease rnds and finish as for ring finger.

Index Finger

Transfer first 7 and last 7 sts from holder to 2 needles. Join yarn at base of middle finger. Pick up and knit 1 st from CO st at base of middle finger, k14 to end—15 sts. Divide sts on 3 needles and work in St st for 2½" (6.5 cm) or ½" (1.3 cm) less than desired length of finger. Work decrease rnds and finish as for ring finger.

Thumb

Transfer 20 sts from thumb holder to 2 needles. Join yarn at base of sts CO for hand. Pick up and knit 2 sts from hand CO, knit to end—22 sts. Divide sts as evenly as possible on 3 needles and work in St st, decreasing 1 st at beginning and end of first rnd—20 sts. Work even in St st until thumb measures 3" (7.5 cm) from sts picked up from hand. Dec Rnd 1: *K1, k2tog; rep from * to last 2 sts, end k2—14 sts. Work 1 rnd even. Dec Rnd 2: K2tog around—7 sts. Finish as for little finger.

Work second glove same as the first.

Fingerless Option

Work as for gloves given above, but make each finger only 1" (2.5 cm) long, then loosely BO each finger's sts. For snug fit, work the thumb gusset and hand in St st, then work the partial fingers in k1, p1 rib. For a classic fingerless glove look, use "rag wool" two-tone marled yarn.

Garter Stitch Aran Pullover

ॐ

This pullover is also known as the "latte" sweater, both for its creamy coffee color and its stylish café mood. A good introduction to paneled Aran knitting, the sweater features three basic elements: garter stitch, basic rope cables, and diamonds filled with garter stitch. For a contemporary look, bands of garter stitch replace traditional ribbing. Knitted here in a machine-washable wool, the Garter Stitch Aran Pullover exudes a casual chic with its easy fit. This sweater is great for Young Men's/Active Casual and Young Professional/Modern Casual style types. Choose it for the following fit issues: *Full physique, and men of Short Stature, Waist, and Neck.*

SPECIFICATIONS

Finished Sizes	Yarn	Needles	Notions	Gauge
Adult S (M, L, XL). 42 (44 ½, 50, 54)" (106.5 [113, 127, 137] cm) finished chest. 24 (25, 26, 27)" (61 [63.5, 66, 68.5] cm) finished length. Sweater shown in size M.	Dale of Norway Freestyle (100% wool; 88 yds [80 m]/50 g): #2611 wheat, 18 (19, 22, 24) skeins.	Size 8 (5 mm): straight. Size 7 (4.5 mm): straight and 16" (40-cm) circ. Adjust needle size if necessary to obtain the correct gauge.	Stitch markers; stitch holders; darning needle; cable needle (cn); scissors; measuring tape; crochet hook G (4.5 mm) for picking up stitches (optional).	Using larger needles, 18 sts and 28 rows = 4" (10 cm) in garter stitch (knit all sts every row). 12-st cable panels measure 1⅞" (4.8 cm) wide, and 25-st center diamond measures 4½" (11.5 cm) wide. Check your gauge before you begin.

Back

With smaller needles, CO 108 (114, 126, 136) sts. Work in garter st for 9 rows. Change to larger needles. On the next row (WS), set up patterns as follows, increasing sts and placing markers (pm) between each st panel where indicated:

K10 (13, 19, 24) garter st, pm;

K1, p1, k2, p2, M1, p1, k2, p1, k1 (left cable), pm;

K5 garter st, pm;

K1, p1, k2, p2, M1, p1, k2, p1, k1 (left cable), pm;

K5 garter st, pm;

K1, p1, k8, p2, M1, p2, k8, p1, k1 (center diamond), pm;

K5 garter st, pm;

K1, p1, k2, p2, M1, p1, k2, p1, k1 (right cable), pm;

K5 garter st, pm;

K1, p1, k2, p2, M1, p1, k2, p1, k1 (right cable), pm;

K10 (13, 19, 24) garter st—113 (119, 131, 141) sts.

On the next row (RS), work in garter st or Row 1 from each chart as follows: 10 (13, 19, 24) sts garter st, 12 sts right cable, 5 sts garter st, 12 sts right cable, 5 sts garter st, 25 sts center diamond, 5 sts garter st, 12 sts left cable, 5 sts garter st, 12 sts left cable, 10 (13, 19, 24) sts garter st. Work even in patterns as established until piece measures 14 (14½, 15, 15½)" (35.5 [37, 38, 39.5] cm) from beginning, ending with a WS row. Armhole shaping: BO 2 sts at beg of next 2 rows—109 (115, 127, 137) sts. Work even in patterns until piece measures 23 (24, 25, 26)" (58.5 [61, 63.5, 66] cm) from beginning, ending with a WS row. Shape back neck: Work 30 (32, 38, 42) sts in pattern, join new ball of yarn, BO center 49 (51, 51, 53) sts, work in pattern to end. Working each side separately, work even in pattern until piece measures 24 (25, 26, 27)" (61 [63.5, 66, 68.5] cm) from beginning. Place 30 (32, 38, 42) sts for each shoulder on separate holders.

Front

Work as for back until piece measures 21 (22, 23, 24)" (53.5 [56, 58.5, 61] cm) from beginning, ending with a WS row. Shape front neck: Work 45 (47, 53, 57) sts in pattern, join new ball of yarn, BO center 19 (21, 21, 23) sts, work in pat-

tern to end. Working each side separately, decrease 1 st at each neck edge every row 10 times, then decrease 1 st at each neck edge every other row 5 times—30 (32, 38, 42) sts. Work even in pattern until piece measures 24 (25, 26, 27)" (61 [63.5, 66, 68.5] cm) from beginning. Place 30 (32, 38, 42) sts for each shoulder on separate holders.

Sleeves

Matching right front and back shoulders, with right sides of fabric held together, join right shoulder using three-needle bind-off technique. Repeat for left shoulder. With RS facing, using larger needles, beginning at inner corner of armhole notch, pick up and knit 98 (102, 106, 110) sts evenly from one armhole notch to the other (using crochet hook for assistance, if desired). On the next row (WS), set up patterns as follows, increasing and placing markers between each st panel where indicated:

K29 (31, 33, 35) garter st, pm;

K1, p1, k2, p2, M1, p1, k2, p1, k1 (left cable), pm;

K1, p2, k6, M1, k6, p2, k1 (center diamond), pm;

K1, p1, k2, p2, M1, p1, k2, p1, k1 (right cable), pm;

K29 (31, 33, 35) garter st—101 (105, 109, 113) sts.

On the next row (RS), work in garter st or indicated

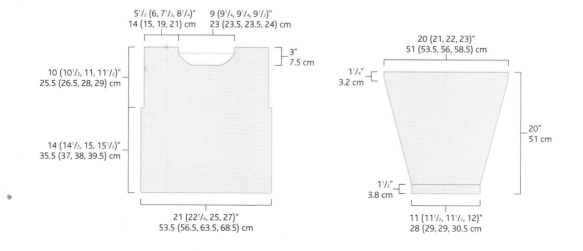

5½ (6, 7½, 8¼)"
14 (15, 19, 21) cm

9 (9¼, 9¼, 9½)"
23 (23.5, 23.5, 24) cm

3"
7.5 cm

10 (10½, 11, 11½)"
25.5 (26.5, 28, 29) cm

14 (14½, 15, 15½)"
35.5 (37, 38, 39.5) cm

21 (22¼, 25, 27)"
53.5 (56.5, 63.5, 68.5) cm

20 (21, 22, 23)"
51 (53.5, 56, 58.5) cm

1¼"
3.2 cm

20"
51 cm

1½"
3.8 cm

11 (11½, 11½, 12)"
28 (29, 29, 30.5 cm

row from each chart as follows: 29 (31, 33, 35) sts garter st, 12 sts right cable Row 1, 19 indicated center sts from center diamond chart Row 19, 12 sts left cable Row 1, 29 (31, 33, 35) sts garter st. Work even in patterns for 7 rows—piece measures approximately 1¼" (3.2 cm) from edge of body. Shape sleeve: Beginning with the next row (RS), decrease 1 st at each side every 6 rows 17 (15, 11, 9) times, then every 4 rows 3 (6, 12, 15) times—61 (63, 63, 65) sts. Work even until piece measures 18½" (47 cm) from pickup row, or 1½" (3.8 cm) less than desired length, ending with a WS row. Change to smaller needles. On the next row (RS), knit across all sts, decreasing 11 sts evenly—50 (52, 52, 54) sts. Work even in garter st for 1½" (3.8 cm). BO all sts loosely as if to knit.

Finishing

Lightly steam block only if needed; blocking can compromise the rich texture of the Aran knitting you have worked so hard to achieve. Sew straight sections at top of sleeves to armhole notches. Sew sleeve and side seams, carefully matching garter st cuffs and bottom borders at sides. Weave in ends.

Neckband

With smaller 16" (40-cm) circ needle, with RS facing and beginning at left shoulder seam, pickup and knit 87 (90, 90, 94) sts evenly around neck opening as follows (using crochet hook for assistance, if desired): 15 sts along side of left front neck, 18 (20, 20, 22) sts across center front, 15 sts along side of right front neck, 39 (40, 40, 42) sts across back neck. Join for working in the round (rnd), and pm to indicate beginning of rnd. Work garter st in the rnd (purl 1 rnd, knit 1 rnd) for 1½" (3.8 cm), or desired length for neckband, ending with a purl rnd. BO all sts loosely as if to knit on next rnd. Weave in ends.

knit on RS; purl on WS

purl on RS; knit on WS

sl 2 sts to cn and hold in back
k2, k2 from cn

sl 2 sts to cn and hold in front,
k2, k2 from cn

sl 1 st to cn and hold in back,
k2, k1 from cn

sl 2 sts to cn and hold in front,
k1, k2 from cn

sl 1 st to cn and hold in back
k2, p1 from cn

sl 2 sts to cn and hold in front,
p1, k2 from cn

sl 3 sts to cn and hold in back,
k2, sl 3rd st from cn to left needle
and purl it, k2 from cn

Left Cable ### Right Cable

Center Diamond

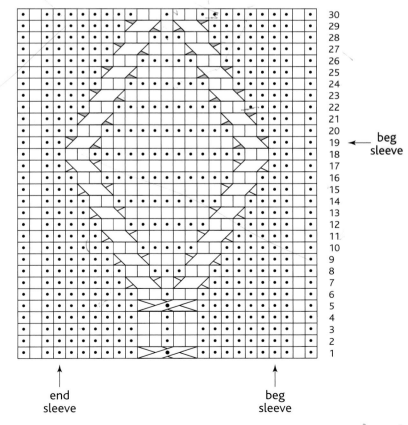

Classic Camel Vest, with Muffler

As the name states, this one is never going out of style. The soft and supple vest is knitted in a luxurious natural color camel and merino blend, and it will appeal to both the Corporate/Traditionalist and the Young Professional/Modern Casual guy. Easy to knit in stockinette stitch with single cable accents up each side of the center front, this timeless classic is a good choice for the following fit issues: *Athletic and Full physiques, Short, Barrel-Chested, Broad Shoulders.* The muffler is a great coordinate to the Classic Camel Vest or a lovely gift on its own. The ribbed cable pattern appears on both sides, so the muffler is reversible.

SPECIFICATIONS

Finished Sizes	Yarn	Needles	Notions	Gauge
Adult S (M, L, XL). 40 (43, 48, 52)" (101.5 [109, 122, 132] cm) finished chest. 24 (25, 26, 27)" (61 [63.5, 66, 68.5] cm) finished length. Vest shown in size M. Muffler approximately 7" x 35½" (18 x 90 cm).	Galler Yarns Sahara (50% camel, 50% Merino wool; 250 yds [229 m]/4 oz [114 g]): natural camel, 3 (4, 4, 5) skeins for vest; 2 skeins for muffler.	Size 7 (4.5 mm): straight or 29" (70-cm) circular (circ). Size 5 (3.75 mm): straight or 29" (70-cm) circ. Size 6 (4 mm) 16" (40-cm) circ. Adjust needle size if necessary to obtain the correct gauge.	Stitch markers; stitch holders; darning needle; cable needle (cn); scissors; measuring tape; five ³/₄-inch (2-cm) buttons (shown: One World Button Supply, NPL 214-20 Coconut Husk 20 mm), crochet hook G (4.5 mm) for picking up stitches (optional).	Using largest needles, 20 sts and 28 rows = 4" (10 cm) in Stockinette stitch (St st); 8-st cable patterns for vest measure 1¹/₈" (2.9 cm) wide, relaxed. Using largest needles 15 sts = 2" 5 cm) in rib cable pattern for muffler. Check your gauge before you begin.

Ssp (slip, slip, purl): Slip 2 sts to right needle one at a time as if to knit, return sts to left needle in their new orientation, and purl 2 together through the back loops.

Back

With smallest straight or circ needles, CO 100 (108, 120, 130) sts. Work in k1, p1 rib for 1½" (3.8 cm) or desired length for rib. Change to larger needles and work in St st until piece measures 13½ (14, 15, 15½)" (34.5 [35.5, 38, 39.5] cm) from beginning, ending with a WS row. Armhole shaping: BO 6 (7, 8, 9) sts at beg of next 2 rows—88 (94, 104, 112) sts remain. Beginning with the next RS row, dec 1 st each at each side every other row 5 (6, 7, 8) times—78 (82, 90, 96) sts. Work even in pattern until piece measures 23½ (24½, 25½, 26½)" (59.5 [62, 65, 67.5] cm) from beginning, ending with a WS row. Shape back neck: Work 20 (20, 23, 25) sts in pattern, join new ball of yarn, BO center 38

(42, 44, 46) sts, work in pattern to end. Working each side separately, work even in pattern until piece measures 24 (25, 26, 27)" (61 [63.5, 66, 68.5] cm) from beginning. Place 20 (20, 23, 25) sts for each shoulder on separate holders.

Left Front

With smallest straight or circ needles, CO 50 (54, 60, 65) sts. Work in k1, p1 rib for 1½" (3.8 cm) or desired length for rib, ending with a RS row. Change to larger needles and establish patterns as follows: (WS) P3, place marker (pm), k2, p4, k2, pm, p39 (43, 49, 54). On the next row (RS), work 39 (43, 49, 54) sts in St st, slip marker (sl m), work 8 sts from Row 1 of left cable chart, sl m, work 3 sts in St st. Work even in patterns as established until piece measures 13½ (14, 15, 15½)" (34.5 [35.5, 38, 39.5] cm) from beginning, ending with a WS row. Armhole shaping: BO 6 (7, 8, 9) sts at beg of next RS row—44 (47, 52, 56) sts remain. Beginning with the next RS row, dec 1 st each at armhole edge (beginning of RS rows) every other row 5 (6, 7, 8) times—39 (41, 45, 48) sts. Work even in patterns until piece measures 16 (17, 18, 18½)" (40.5 [43, 45.5, 47] cm) from beginning, ending with a WS row. Shape V neck: On the next row (RS), work to last knit st before cable panel, ssp (last knit st and first purl st of cable panel; remove m the first time you work this decrease), work remaining 7 sts of left cable pattern, k3—1 st decreased. Work 1 WS row even. Repeat the last 2 rows 18 (20, 21, 22) more times, decreasing 1 st at beginning of cable panel on RS rows as given above—20 (20, 23, 25) sts. Work even if necessary until piece measures 24 (25, 26, 27)" (61 [63.5, 66, 68.5] cm) from beginning. Place sts on holder.

Right Front

With smallest straight or circ needles, CO 50 (54, 60, 65) sts. Work in k1, p1 rib for 1½" (3.8 cm) or desired length for rib, ending with a RS row. Change to larger needles and establish patterns as follows: (WS) P39 (43, 49, 54), pm, k2, p4, k2, pm, p3. On the next row (RS), work 3 sts in St st, slip marker (sl m), work 8 sts from Row 1 of right cable chart, sl m, work 39 (43, 49, 54) sts in St st. Work even in patterns as established until piece measures 13½ (14, 15, 15½)" (34.5 [35.5, 38, 39.5] cm) from beginning, ending with a RS row. Armhole shaping: BO 6 (7, 8, 9) sts at beg of next WS row—44 (47, 52, 56) sts remain. Beginning with the next RS row, dec 1 st each at armhole edge (end of RS rows) every other row 5 (6, 7, 8) times—39 (41, 45, 48) sts. Work even in patterns until piece measures 16 (17, 18, 18½)" (40.5 [43, 45.5, 47] cm) from beginning, ending with a WS row. Shape V neck: On the next row (RS), k3, work first 7 sts of cable panel, p2tog (last purl st of cable panel and first knit st after it; remove m the first time you work this decrease), work in St st to end—1 st decreased. Work 1 WS row even. Repeat the last

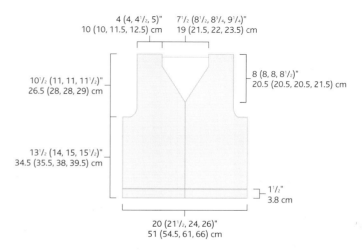

4 (4, 4½, 5)"
10 (10, 11.5, 12.5) cm

7½ (8½, 8¾, 9¼)"
19 (21.5, 22, 23.5) cm

10½ (11, 11, 11½)"
26.5 (28, 28, 29) cm

8 (8, 8, 8½)"
20.5 (20.5, 20.5, 21.5) cm

13½ (14, 15, 15½)"
34.5 (35.5, 38, 39.5) cm

1½"
3.8 cm

20 (21½, 24, 26)"
51 (54.5, 61, 66) cm

2 rows 18 (20, 21, 22) more times, decreasing 1 st at end of cable panel on RS rows as given above—20 (20, 23, 25) sts. Work even if necessary until piece measures 24 (25, 26, 27)" (61 [63.5, 66, 68.5] cm) from beginning. Place sts on holder.

Finishing

Matching right front and back shoulders, with right sides facing, join right shoulder using three-needle bind-off technique. Repeat for left shoulder. Lightly steam block only if needed. Sew side seams. Weave in ends.

Front Band

Mark positions on left front for five evenly spaced buttonholes, the lowest located ½" (1.3 cm) up from bottom edge, and the highest ½" (1.3 cm) below the beginning of the V-neck shaping. With RS facing and using smallest circ needle, beginning at bottom edge of right front, pick up and knit 262 (278, 288, 300) sts around front opening as follows (using crochet hook for assistance, if desired): 71 (76, 80, 82) sts from bottom edge to beginning of V-neck shaping, 40 (40, 40, 43) sts from beginning of V-neck shaping to shoulder seam, 40 (46, 48, 50) sts across back neck, 40 (40, 40, 43) sts from left shoulder seam to beginning of V-neck shaping, 71 (76, 80, 82) sts from V-neck shaping to bottom edge. Work in k1, p1 rib for 2 rows. On the next row (WS), make five 2-row buttonholes as follows: *Work in rib pattern to marked buttonhole position, BO 2 sts; repeat from * 4 more times, work in rib pattern to end. On the next row (RS), CO 2 sts above each gap in the buttonhole row to complete buttonholes. Work 3 more rows. BO all sts loosely in rib pattern on next row. Weave in ends. Sew buttons to right front to correspond to buttonholes.

Ribbed Cable

knit on RS; purl on WS

• purl on RS; knit on WS

pattern repeat

sl 2 sts to cn and hold in back, k2, k2 from cn

sl 2 sts to cn and hold in front, k2, k2 from cn

sl 6 sts to cn and hold in back, (k1, p1) 3 times, (k1, p1) 3 times from cn

sl 6 sts to cn and hold in front, (p1, k1) 3 times, (p1, k1) 3 times from cn

Left Cable

Right Cable

Armhole Finishing

With RS facing and using medium-size 16" (40-cm) circ needle, beginning at underarm seam, pick up and knit 112 (118, 120, 126) sts evenly around armhole edge, (using crochet hook for assistance, if desired). Join for working in the round (rnd) and work in k1, p1 rib for ¾" (2 cm) or desired length. BO all sts loosely in rib on next rnd. Weave in ends. Repeat for other armhole.

Muffler

Using largest needles, CO 63 sts. Work in k1, p1 rib for 2 rows. Work according to ribbed cable chart until piece measures 35¼" (89.5 cm) or slightly less than desired length, ending with Row 7 of chart. Work 2 rows k1, p1 rib. BO all sts loosely. Weave in ends. Block lightly, if desired.

Basketcase Jacket

This sweater is such a snap to knit that you won't go crazy (i.e., turn into a basketcase) creating it. A cuddly, bulky jacket in super-soft wool, this sweater can go weekend casual or act as a jacket for the Modern Casual "new office" look. A real sweater coat, it's perfect for a guy seeking a bulky wear-anywhere garment, and it's a good choice for any Personal Style category and for the following fit issues: *Athletic and Average physiques, the Tall guy, and the really Thin guy.*

SPECIFICATIONS

Finished Sizes	Yarn	Needles	Notions	Gauge
Adult S (M, L/XL). 40 (47, 54)" (101.5 [119.5, 137] cm) finished chest. 25 (26, 28)" (63.5 [66, 71] cm) finished length. Cardigan shown in size M.	Rowan Big Wool (100% wool; 87 yds [80 m]/100 g): #007 smoky, 9 (10, 12) skeins.	Size 15 (10 mm): 29" (70-cm) circular (circ). Size 13 (9 mm): 29" (70-cm) circ. Adjust needle size if necessary to obtain the correct gauge.	Stitch markers; stitch holders; darning needle; scissors; measuring tape; five 1½-inch (3.8-cm) buttons (shown: One World Button Supply, #NPL197-40H Horn Toggle 40 mm), crochet hook M (9 mm) for picking up stitches (optional).	Using larger needles, 9 sts and 12 rows = 4" (10 cm) in basketweave pattern from chart. Check your gauge before you begin.

Back

With smaller needle, CO 42 (50, 58) sts. Work in k2, p2 rib as follows:

Row 1: (RS) *K2, p2; repeat from * to last 2 sts, end k2.

Row 2: (WS) *P2, k2; repeat from * to last 2 sts, end p2.

Repeat these 2 rows until piece measures 3" (7.5 cm) from beginning, ending with a WS row, and increasing 3 sts evenly in last row—45 (53, 61) sts. Change to larger needle. Work basketweave pattern from chart, beginning and ending at outer edges of the chart, until piece measures 13¼ (14¼, 16¼)" (33.5 [36, 41.5] cm)

from beginning, including ribbing, ending with a WS row. Armhole shaping: BO 5 sts at beg of next 2 rows— 35 (43, 51) sts remain. Maintaining pattern as established, work even until piece measures 24½ (25½, 27½)" (62 [65, 70] cm) from beginning, ending with a WS row. Shape back neck: Work 9 (12, 16) sts in pattern, join new ball of yarn, BO center 17 (19, 19) sts, work in pattern to end. Working each side separately, work even in pattern until piece measures 25 (26, 28)" (63.5 [66, 71] cm) from beginning. Place 9 (12, 16) sts for each shoulder on separate holders.

Left Front

With smaller needle, CO 18 (22, 26) sts. Work in k2, p2 rib as for back until piece measures 3" (7.5 cm) from beginning, ending with a WS row, and increasing 3 sts evenly in last row—21 (25, 29) sts. Change to larger needle. Work basketweave pattern from chart, beginning and ending where indicated for left front in your size, until piece measures 13¼ (14¼, 16¼)" (33.5 [36, 41.5] cm) from beginning, including ribbing, ending with a WS row. Armhole shaping: (RS) BO 5 sts at armhole edge at beginning of row, work to end—16 (2), 24) sts. Continue in pattern until piece measures 22 (3, 25)" (56 [58.5, 63.5] cm) from beginning, ending with a RS row. Shape neck: At the beginning of the next row (WS), BO 4 (5, 5) sts—12 (15, 19) sts. Decrease 1 st at neck edge every other row 3 times—9 (12, 16) sts. Maintaining pattern as established, work even until piece measures 25 (26, 28)" (63.5 [66, 71] cm) from beginning. Place sts on holder.

Right Front

Work as for left front, reversing pattern placement by beginning and ending where indicated for right front in your size, and reversing shaping by binding off for armhole at the beginning of a WS row, and binding off for neck at beginning of a RS row. Place sts on holder as for left front.

Sleeves

Matching right front and back shoulders, with right sides of fabric held together, join right shoulder using three-needle bind-off technique. Repeat for left shoulder. With RS facing, using larger needles, beginning at inner corner of armhole notch, pick up and knit 53 sts evenly from one armhole notch to the other (using crochet hook for assistance, if desired). Next row (WS): Purl all sts. Work basketweave pattern from chart, beginning and ending at outer edges of the chart, until sleeve measures 2¼" (5.5 cm) from pickup row. Shape sleeve: Beginning with the next row, decrease 1 st at each side every 4 rows 10 times, then every 2 rows 2 times—29 sts remain. Work even until sleeve measures approximately 17" (43 cm) from pickup row, ending with Row 4 or Row 8 of basketweave pattern, if possible. Change to smaller needles, and work in k2, p2 rib as for back, decreasing 1 st in first row of rib—28 sts. Work even in rib until sleeve measures 20" (51 cm) from pickup row. BO all sts loosely in rib pattern.

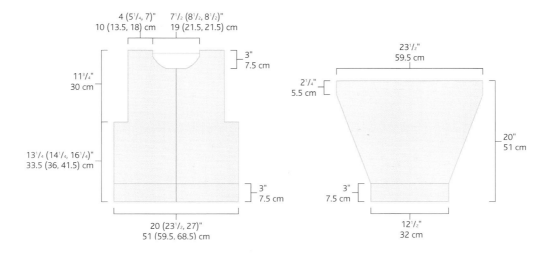

Finishing

Sew straight sections at top of sleeves to armhole notches, sew sleeve and side seams. Weave in ends.

Right Front Band

With RS facing and using smaller circ needle, beginning at bottom edge of right front, pick up and knit 66 (70, 74) sts along center front edge (using crochet hook for assistance, if desired). Establish k2, p2 rib on next row (WS) as follows: *P2, k2; repeat from * to last 2 sts, end p2. For all other rows, knit the knits and purl the purls as they appear, and work in k2, p2 rib for 6 more rows. BO all sts loosely in rib pattern.

Left Front Band

Mark positions on left front for five evenly spaced buttonholes, the lowest located ½" (1.3 cm) up from bottom edge, and the highest ½" (1.3 cm) below the beginning of the neck shaping. With RS facing and using smaller circ needle, beginning at neck edge of left front, pick up and knit 66 (70, 74) sts along center front edge (using crochet hook for assistance, if desired). Work in k2, p2 rib as for right front band for 2 rows. *Note:* Where possible, make the buttonholes in the "purl ditch" of the band, placing the binding off for the buttonhole over 2 RS purl sts of the rib; it is OK to fudge the buttonhole spacing a little if you prefer the neat and tidy effect this creates. On the next row (WS), make five 2-row buttonholes as follows: *Work in rib pattern to marked buttonhole position, BO 2 sts, repeat from * 4 more times, work in rib pattern to end. On the next row (RS), CO 2 sts above each gap in the buttonhole row to complete buttonholes. Work 2 more rows. BO all sts loosely in rib pattern.

Collar

With RS facing and using smaller circ needle, beginning and ending at the center of each front band, pick up and knit 50 (54, 58) sts around neck edge (using crochet hook for assistance, if desired). Work in k2, p2 rib as for front bands until collar measures 3" (7.5 cm), or desired length. BO all sts loosely in rib pattern.

Finishing

Weave in ends. Lightly steam block only if needed. Sew toggle buttons to right front to correspond to buttonholes.

Basketweave Pattern

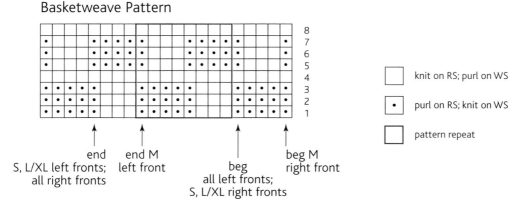

knit on RS; purl on WS

· purl on RS; knit on WS

pattern repeat

Fast Favorite Vest

THE NAME SAYS IT ALL. Knitted in garter stitch rib, these vests work up so fast and easy that they will become a favorite to knit. As wardrobe basics that dress up or down, they'll also be a favorite to wear. Play up a vest using an elegant yarn—such as the shiny and drapey silk blend of the adult vest—to effortlessly transition from work to drinks and dinner. Play it down, using a rustic yarn like the raw silk of the child's version. It is perfect for a special occasion, but not too far out of the realm of everyday wear. The simple pattern stitch of the Fast Favorite Vest is quick and engaging to knit, so enjoy making both big and little versions.

Fast Favorite Vest—Adult

ༀ

Infused with casual style, this vest is dressed up with a smooth silk-blend yarn that makes it versatile enough for jeans or slacks. The Fast Favorite Vest is an easy pick for the Young Men's/Active Casual category. Knitted in a neutral tone, it will effortlessly coordinate with the wardrobe style of the Young Professional/Modern Casual guy. A smooth vertical style without ribbing provides a relaxed fit and slim line. Choose this pattern for the following fit issues: *All physiques, Short, Short-Waisted, Broad Shoulders, Thin guys.*

SPECIFICATIONS

Finished Sizes	Yarn	Needles	Notions	Gauge
Adult S (M, L, XL). 41 (44½, 48, 51)" (104 [113, 122, 129.5] cm) finished chest. 25 (26, 27, 27½)" (63.5 [66, 68.5, 70] cm) finished length. Vest shown in size S.	Muench Maulbeerseide (50% silk, 50% cotton; 110 yds [100 m]/50 g): #16 blue, 8 (9, 10, 11) balls.	Size 7 (4.5 mm): straight or 29" (70-cm) circular (circ). Size 5 (3.75 mm): 29" (70-cm) and 16" (40-cm) circ. Adjust needle size if necessary to obtain the correct gauge.	Stitch markers; stitch holders; darning needle; scissors; measuring tape; five ⅝" (1.6-cm) buttons (shown: One World Button Supply, Concave Oval Corozo 36 mm, royal blue, SPN-106-36RB), crochet hook G (4.5 mm) for picking up stitches (optional).	Using larger needles, 19 sts and 28 rows = 4" (10 cm) in garter rib pattern from chart. Check your gauge before you begin.

Back

With straight needles or larger 29" (70-cm) circ needle, CO 98 (106, 114, 122) sts. Work even in garter rib pattern from chart until piece measures 14 (14½, 15½, 16)" (35.5 [37, 39.5, 40.5] cm) or desired length to underarm ending with a WS row. Armhole shaping: BO 5 (6, 8, 10) sts at beg of next 2 rows—88 (94, 98, 102) sts remain. Beginning with the next RS row, dec 1 st each at each side every other row 5 (7, 8, 9) times—78 (80, 82, 84) sts. Work even in pattern until piece meas-

ures 24½ (25½, 26½, 27)" (62 [65, 67.5, 68.5] cm), ending with a WS row. Shape back neck: Work 21 (22, 22, 22) sts in pattern, join second ball of yarn, BO center 36 (36, 38, 40) sts, work to end. Working each side separately, work even until piece measures 25 (26, 27, 27½)" (63.5 [66, 68.5, 70] cm) from beginning. Place 21 (22, 22, 22) sts for each shoulder on separate holders.

Left Front

With straight needles or larger 29" (70-cm) circ nee-

dle, CO 46 (50, 54, 58) sts. Work even in garter rib pattern from chart until piece measures 14 (14½, 15½, 16)" (35.5 [37, 39.5, 40.5] cm) or desired length to underarm ending with a WS row. Shape armhole and V neck: (RS) BO 5 (6, 8, 10) sts at armhole edge at beginning of row, work to end—41 (44, 46, 48) sts. Beginning with the next RS row, dec 1 st at armhole edge every other row 5 (7, 8, 9) times, and *at the same time,* when piece measures 16½ (17½, 18½, 19)" (42 [44.5, 47, 48.5] cm) from beginning, shape V neck by dec 1 st at neck edge every 3 rows 15 (15, 16, 17) times—21 (22, 22, 22) sts remain. Work even until piece measures 25 (26, 27, 27½)" (63.5 [66, 68.5, 70] cm) from beginning. Place sts on holder.

Right Front

Work as for left front, reversing shaping by beginning armhole shaping on a WS row. Place sts on holder as for left front.

Finishing

Matching right front and back shoulders, with right sides facing, join right shoulder using three-needle bind-off technique. Repeat for left shoulder. Lightly steam block only if needed. Sew side seams. Weave in ends.

Front Band

Mark positions on left front for five evenly spaced buttonholes, the lowest located ½" (1.3 cm) up from bottom edge, and the highest ½" (1.3 cm) below the beginning of the V-neck shaping. With RS facing and using smaller 29" (70-cm) circ needle, beg at bottom edge of right front, pick up and knit 266 (272, 280, 284) sts around front opening as follows (using crochet hook for assistance, if

desired): 70 (73, 75, 77) sts from bottom edge to beginning of V-neck shaping, 43 sts from beginning of V-neck shaping to shoulder seam, 40 (40, 44, 44) sts along back neck, 43 sts from left shoulder seam to beginning of V-neck shaping, 70 (73, 75, 77) sts from V-neck shaping to bottom edge. Knit 2 rows. On the next row (WS), make five 2-row buttonholes as follows: *Knit to marked buttonhole position, BO 2 sts; repeat from * 4 more times, knit to end. On the next row, CO 2 sts above each gap in the previous row to complete buttonholes. Knit 3 rows— 7 rows total. BO all sts loosely. Weave in ends. Sew buttons to right front to correspond to buttonholes.

Armhole Finishing

With RS facing and using 16" (40-cm) circ needle, beginning at underarm seam, pick up and knit 130 (140, 148, 152) sts evenly around armhole edge, (using crochet hook for assistance, if desired). Join for working in the round and loosely BO all sts as if to knit on next round. Weave in ends. Repeat for other armhole.

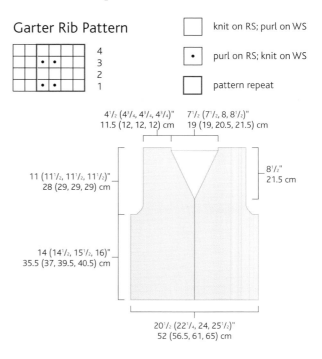

Garter Rib Pattern

						4
		•	•			3
						2
		•	•			1

☐ knit on RS; purl on WS

• purl on RS; knit on WS

☐ pattern repeat

4½ (4¾, 4¾, 4¾)"
11.5 (12, 12, 12) cm

7½ (7½, 8, 8½)"
19 (19, 20.5, 21.5) cm

8½"
21.5 cm

11 (11½, 11½, 11½)"
28 (29, 29, 29) cm

14 (14½, 15½, 16)"
35.5 (37, 39.5, 40.5) cm

20½ (22¼, 24, 25½)"
52 (56.5, 61, 65) cm

Fast Favorite Vest—Child

For this child's version of the easy-to-knit and easy-to-wear Fast Favorite Vest, yarn choice can considerably affect the garment's versatility. Here, a raw silk in a neutral tone results in a casual look that dresses up or down depending on the rest of the outfit.

SPECIFICATIONS

Finished Sizes

Child S (M, L), to fit 4 (6/8, 10/12) years. 31 (34½, 38)" (78.5 [87.5, 96.5] cm) finished chest. 16 (17, 19)" (40.5 [43, 48.5] cm) finished length. Vest shown in size L, to fit 10/12 years.

Yarn

Plymouth Turino Silk (100% silk; 105 yds [96 m]/50 g): #07 gray, 5 (6, 7) balls.

Needles

Size 6 (4 mm): straight or 29" (70-cm) circular (circ), and 16" (40-cm) circ. Adjust needle size if necessary to obtain the correct gauge.

Notions

Stitch markers; stitch holders; darning needle; scissors; measuring tape; five ½" (1.3-cm) buttons (shown: One World Button Supply, Rough Horn Tablet 20 mm, NPL237-20H), crochet hook G (4 mm) for picking up stitches (optional).

Gauge

19 sts and 28 rows = 4" (10 cm) in garter rib pattern from chart. Check your gauge before you begin.

Back

With straight needles or longer circ needle, CO 74 (82, 90) sts. Work even in garter rib pattern from chart until piece measures 9 (10, 12)" (23 [25.5, 30.5] cm) or desired length to underarm ending with a WS row. Armhole shaping: BO 5 sts at beg of next 2 rows—64 (72, 80) sts remain. Beginning with the next RS row, dec 1 st each at each side every other row 6 (8, 11) times—52 (56, 58) sts. Work even in pattern until piece measures 15¾ (16¾, 18¾)" (40 [42.5, 47.5] cm), ending with a WS row. Shape back neck: Work 12 (14, 14) sts in pattern, join second ball of yarn, BO center 28 (28, 30) sts, work to end. Working each side separately, work even until piece measures 16 (17, 19)" (40.5 [43, 48.5] cm) from beginning. Place 12 (14, 14) sts for each shoulder on separate holders.

Left Front

With straight needles or longer circ needle, CO 34 (38, 42) sts. Work even in garter rib pattern from chart until piece measures 9 (10, 12)" (23 [25.5, 30.5] cm) or desired length to underarm ending with a WS row. Shape armhole and V neck: (RS) BO 5 sts at armhole edge at beginning of row, work in pattern

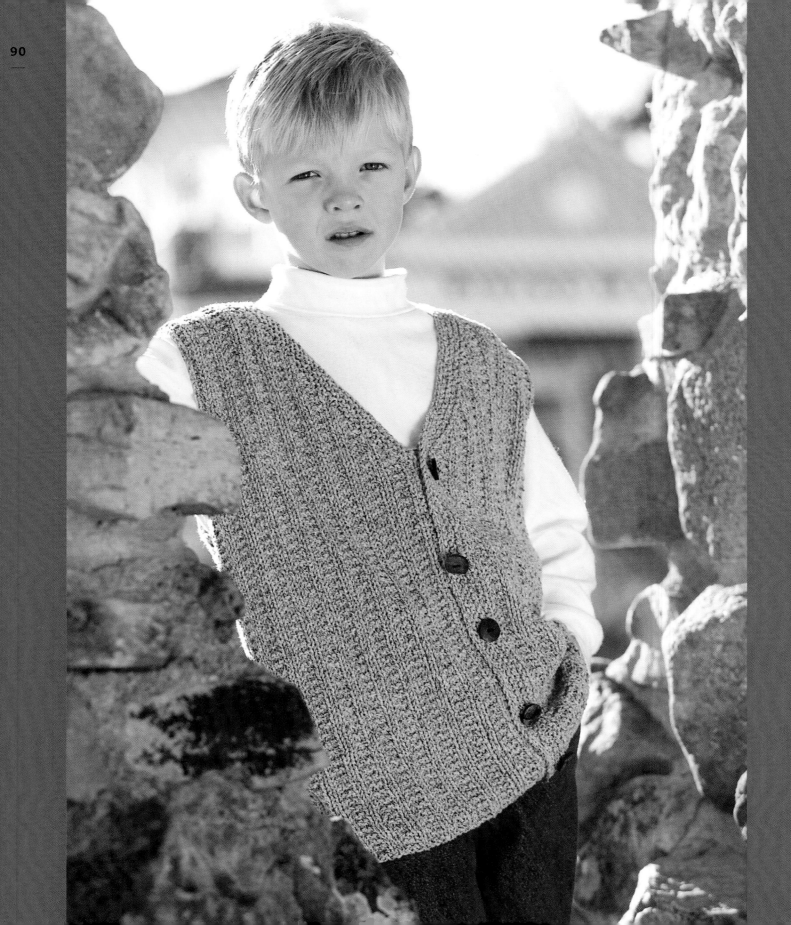

to last 3 sts, work 2 sts together in pattern, work last st—28 (32, 36) sts. Continue in pattern, and at the same time, dec 1 st at armhole edge every other row 5 (7, 10) more times, and decrease 1 st at V-neck edge as before every other row 6 times, then every 3 rows 5 (5, 6) times—12 (14, 14) sts rem. Work even until piece measures 16 (17, 19)" (40.5 [43, 48.5] cm) from beginning. Place sts on holder.

Right Front

Work as for left front, reversing shaping by beginning armhole and V-neck shaping on a WS row. Place sts on holder as for left front.

Finishing

Matching right front and back shoulders, with right sides facing, join right shoulder using three-needle bind-off technique. Repeat for left shoulder. Lightly steam block only if needed. Sew side seams. Weave in ends.

Front Band

Mark positions on left front for five evenly spaced buttonholes, the lowest located ½" (1.3 cm) up from bottom edge, and the highest ½" (1.3 cm) below the beginning of the V-neck shaping. With RS facing and using longer circ needle, beg at bottom edge of right front, pick up and knit 202 (212, 234) sts around front opening as follows (using crochet hook for assistance, if desired): 52 (57, 67) sts from bottom edge to beginning of V-neck shaping, 34 sts from beginning of V-neck shaping to shoulder seam, 30 (30, 32) sts along back neck, 34 sts from left shoulder seam to beginning of V-neck shaping, 52 (57, 67) sts from V-neck shaping to bottom edge. Knit 3 rows. On the next row (RS), make five 2-row buttonholes as follows: *Knit to marked buttonhole position, BO 2 sts; repeat from * 4 more times, knit to end. On the next row, CO 2 sts above each gap in the previous row to complete buttonholes. Knit 1 row—7 rows total for front band, including pick-up row. BO all sts loosely. Weave in ends. Sew buttons to right front to correspond to buttonholes.

Armhole Finishing

With RS facing and using shorter circ needle, beginning at underarm seam, pick up and knit 67 (71, 75) sts evenly around armhole edge (using crochet hook for assistance, if desired). Join for working in the round and loosely BO all sts as if to knit on next round. Weave in ends. Repeat for other armhole.

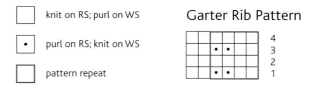

knit on RS; purl on WS

• purl on RS; knit on WS

pattern repeat

Garter Rib Pattern

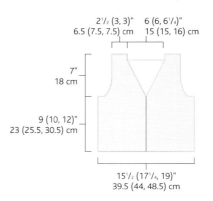

Rustic Raglan Pullover

This warm, chunky raglan pullover is knitted from the top down and features a bulky, slubby yarn with a hint of marled color. Soft and comfortable, it's a hands-down winner for the Young Men's/Active Casual guy. Knitted in a neutral creamy tone, the sweater moves easily into the wardrobe of the Young Professional/Modern Casual or the weekend gear of the Corporate/Traditionalist. Choose this pattern for the following body types and fit issues: *Athletic physique, Tall, and Broad Shoulders.*

SPECIFICATIONS

Finished Sizes	Yarn	Needles	Notions	Gauge
Adult S (M, L, XL). 42½ (46½, 49, 53)" (108 [118, 124.5, 134.5] cm) finished chest. 25 (25, 27, 28½)" (63.5 [63.5, 68.5, 72.5] cm) finished length. Sweater shown in size L.	Dale Ara (100% wool; 55 yds [50 m]/50 g): #404 cream, 17 (18, 20, 23) skeins.	Size 11 (8 mm): 29" (70-cm) and 16" (40-cm) circular (circ), and double pointed (dpn). Size 10 (6 mm): 16" (40-cm) circ and dpn. Adjust needle size if necessary to obtain the correct gauge.	Stitch markers; stitch holders; darning needle; scissors; measuring tape; crochet hook L (8 mm) for picking up stitches (optional).	Using larger needles, 12 sts and 16 rows = 4" (10 cm) in Stockinette st (St st). Check your gauge before you begin.

Note: This project is worked from the top down.

Neckband

With smaller 16" (40-cm) circ, CO 64 (64, 72, 72) sts. Join, being careful not to twist, and place marker (pm) to indicate beginning of round (rnd). Work even in St st for 6 rnds for rolled edge. Change to k2, p2 rib and work in rib for 2½" (6.5 cm) or desired length for neckband. Knit 1 rnd even.

Yoke

The yoke rnds begin at the back left shoulder. On the next rnd, establish yoke patterns as follows: P1, k2, p1 (seam sts), pm, k6 (6, 8, 8) sts for left sleeve, pm, p1, k2, p1, pm, k18 (18, 20, 20) sts for front, pm, p1, k2, p1, pm, k6 (6, 8, 8) sts for right sleeve, pm, p1, k2, p1, pm, k18 (18, 20, 20) sts for back, pm. *Note:* You may find it helpful to use a different-colored marker to indicate the beginning of the rnd. Increase rnd: *Work 4 seam sts as established, slip marker (sl m), make 1 st (M1), work to next m, M1, sl m; repeat from * 3 more times; the last marker you come to should be the end of rnd marker—8 sts increased. Work increase rnd every rnd 7 (11, 11, 13) more times, then work increase

rnd every other rnd 13 (12, 13, 14) times, changing to larger 29" (70-cm) needle when necessary—232 (256, 272, 296) sts. Yoke measures about 9 (9½, 10, 11)" (23 [24, 25.5, 28] cm) from base of neckband, measured vertically along a single column of sts.

Divide for Sleeves and Body

Note: You may find it helpful to use lengths of scrap yarn to hold the sleeve sts. On the next rnd, divide for sleeves and body, removing yoke markers as you work. Place 56 (62, 66, 72) sts on holder for left sleeve (48 [54, 58, 64] sleeve sts, plus 4 seam sts at each side of sleeve), using cable cast-on CO 2 sts at underarm, pm, CO 2 sts, knit across 60 (66, 70, 76) sts for front, place next 56 (62, 66, 72) sts on holder for right sleeve (48 [54, 58, 64] sleeve sts, plus 4 seam sts at each side of sleeve), CO 2 sts, pm, CO 2 sts, knit across 60 (66, 70, 76) sts for back—128 (140, 148, 160) sts on needle for body; 56 (62, 66, 72) sts each on two holders for sleeves.

Body

The body rnds begin at the left side marker. Work even on 128 (140, 148, 160) sts until piece measures 13 (12½, 14, 14½)" (33 [31.5, 35.5, 37] cm) or 3" (7.5 cm) less than desired length from underarm. Change to smaller circ needle and work in k2, p2 rib for 2½" (6.5 cm). Work even in St st for 6 rnds, or desired length of rolled edge. BO all sts loosely.

Sleeves

Place 56 (62, 66, 72) sts for left sleeve on larger 16" (40-cm) circ needle. Join yarn with RS facing. Knit across all sts, pick up and knit 2 sts from the sts CO at underarm for body, pm, pick up 2 more sts from sts CO at underarm for body—60 (66, 70, 76) sts. Beginning of rnd is at the marker. Work in St st, and beginning with the next rnd, decrease 1 st on either side of marker every 5 (4, 4, 4) rnds 5 (12, 14, 5) times, then every 4 (3, 3, 3) rnds 9 (5, 3, 15) times, changing to larger dpn when necessary—32 (32, 36, 36) sts. Work even until sleeve measures 16 (16½, 17, 17)" (40.5 [42, 43, 43] cm) from underarm, or 3" (7.5 cm) less than desired length. Change to smaller dpn and work in k2, p2 rib for 2½" (6.5 cm). Work even in St st for 6 rnds, or desired length of rolled edge. BO all sts loosely.

Finishing

Lightly steam block only if needed. Weave in ends.

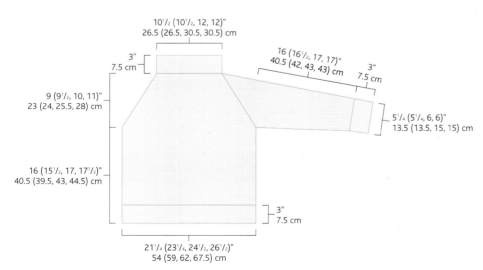

10½ (10½, 12, 12)"
26.5 (26.5, 30.5, 30.5) cm

3"
7.5 cm

16 (16½, 17, 17)"
40.5 (42, 43, 43) cm

3"
7.5 cm

9 (9½, 10, 11)"
23 (24, 25.5, 28) cm

5¼ (5¼, 6, 6)"
13.5 (13.5, 15, 15) cm

16 (15½, 17, 17½)"
40.5 (39.5, 43, 44.5) cm

3"
7.5 cm

21¼ (23¼, 24½, 26½)"
54 (59, 62, 67.5) cm

Fred's Jazz Vest

☙

This fast-knitting, hip take on a classic vest silhouette features a yarn called "Jazz," and I've named the sweater after my favorite jazz man—my dad, tenor saxophonist Fred Hess. Featuring striped accents across the chest, the vest is worked in the round and joined at the shoulders with a three-needle bind-off that leaves no seams to sew. Knitted in a multi-toned alpaca yarn, Fred's Jazz Vest is soft and warm but won't overheat its wearer during active pursuits. This style best suits the Young Men's/Active Casual and Young Professional/Modern Casual Personal Styles and is a good pick for the following fit issues: *Athletic physique, Tall, and Broad/Square Shoulders.*

SPECIFICATIONS

Finished Sizes	Yarn	Needles	Notions	Gauge
Adult S (M, L, XL). 40 (43, 49, 53)" (101.5 [109, 124.5, 134.5] cm) finished chest. 24 (25, 26, 26)" (61 [63.5, 66, 66] cm) finished length. Vest shown in size M.	Artful Yarns Jazz (50% alpaca, 50% wool; 246 yds [225 m]/150 g): #55 Miles Davis (MC; blue, green, gold mix), 3 (3, 4, 4) skeins. Reynolds Andean Alpaca Regal (90% alpaca, 10% wool; 110 yds [100 m]/100 g): #19 Teal (C1) and #08 Brass (C2), 1 skein each.	Size 9 (5.5 mm): 29" (70-cm) circular (circ). Size 7 (4.5 mm): 29" (70-cm) and 16" (40 cm) circ. Adjust needle size if necessary to obtain the correct gauge.	Stitch markers; stitch holders; darning needle; scissors; measuring tape; crochet hook I (5.5 mm) for picking up stitches (optional).	Using larger needles, 16 sts and 23 rows = 4" (10 cm) in Stockinette stitch (St st). Check your gauge before you begin.

Body

With smaller 29" (70-cm) circ needle and MC, CO 152 (164, 186, 202) sts. Join, being careful not to twist, and place marker (pm) to indicate beginning of round (rnd). Work in k1, p1 rib for 2 rnds. Change to C1 and knit 1 rnd. Change to MC and work 8 rnds in k1, p1 rib, increasing 9 (9, 11, 11) sts evenly in last rnd—161 (173, 197, 213) sts. Change to larger 29" (70-cm) circ needle. Work even in St st until piece measures 10¾ (11¼,12¼, 12¼)"

(27.5 [28.5, 31, 31] cm) from beginning. Work accent stripes as follows: 2 rnds C1, 4 rnds C2, [1 rnd C1, 1 rnd C2] twice, 2 rnds C2—12 accent stripe rnds completed; piece measures about 13 (13½, 14½, 14½)" (33 [34.5, 37, 37] cm) from beginning. On the next rnd, change to MC, and divide for front and back as follows: K73 (75, 85, 93) sts, BO 8 (12, 14, 14) sts, k72 (74, 84, 92) sts, BO 8 (12, 14, 14) sts. The group of sts to be worked next are the sts for the front.

Front

Leaving sts for back unworked on the cable part of the circ needle, work 73 (75, 85, 93 front sts back and forth in rows. Shape armhole: Beginning with the first row (RS), decrease 1 st at each end every other row 5 (3, 6, 6) times—63 (69, 73, 81) sts. Work even until piece measures 2½" (6.5 cm) from underarm dividing rnd, ending with a WS row. Shape V neck: (RS) K31 (34, 36, 40) sts, place center st on holder, join second ball of yarn, k31 (34, 36, 40) sts to end. Working each side separately, decrease 1 st at neck edge every other row 4 (8, 10, 10) times, then every three rows 12 (10, 9, 9) times—15 (16, 17, 21) sts. Work even until piece measures 24 (25, 26, 26)" (61 [63.5, 66, 66] cm) from beginning. Place 15 (16, 17, 21) sts for each shoulder on separate holders.

Back

Join MC to sts on cable needle for back with RS facing—72 (74, 84, 92) sts. Work armhole decreases as for front—62 (68, 72, 80) sts. Work even until piece measures ¼" (0.6 cm) less than front, ending with a WS row. Shape back neck: Knit 15 (16, 17, 21) sts, join second ball of yarn, BO center 32 (36, 38, 38) sts, knit to end. Working each side separately, work even until piece measures 24 (25, 26, 26)" (61 [63.5, 66, 66] cm) from beginning. Place 15 (16, 17, 21) sts for each shoulder on separate holders.

Finishing

Matching right front and back shoulders, with right sides facing, join right shoulder using three-needle bind-off technique. Repeat for left shoulder. Lightly steam block only if needed. Weave in ends.

V-neck Band

Using MC, with RS facing and 16" (40-cm) circ needle, beginning at left shoulder seam, pick up and knit 122 (130, 132, 132) sts around neck opening as follows (using crochet hook for assistance, if desired): 41 (43, 43, 43) sts along left side neck, pm, knit 1 st from center front holder, pm, pick up and knit 41 (43, 43, 43) sts along right side neck, pick up and knit 39 (43, 45, 45) sts across back neck. Next rnd: Work in k1, p1 rib to 2 sts before first marker, ssk, slip marker (sl m), k1 (center st), sl m, k2tog, work in k1, p1 rib to end—120 (128, 130, 130) sts. Work 2 more rnds in this manner, decreasing on either side of center marked st on each rnd—116 (124, 126, 126) sts. Change to C1 and work 1 rnd, decreasing as before—114 (122, 124, 124) sts. Change to MC and work 2 rnds, decreasing as before—110 (118, 120, 120) sts. BO all sts loosely in rib pattern with MC. Weave in ends.

Armhole Bands

Using MC, with RS facing and 16" (40-cm) circ, beginning at base of armhole pick up and knit 96 (100, 100, 100) sts evenly around armhole edge (using crochet hook for assistance, if desired). Join for working in the rnd, and work 4 rnds k1, p1 rib. BO all sts loosely in rib pattern. Weave in ends. Repeat for other armhole.

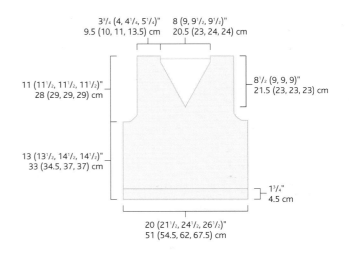

3¾ (4, 4¼, 5¼)"
9.5 (10, 11, 13.5) cm

8 (9, 9½, 9½)"
20.5 (23, 24, 24) cm

11 (11½, 11½, 11½)"
28 (29, 29, 29) cm

8½ (9, 9, 9)"
21.5 (23, 23, 23) cm

13 (13½, 14½, 14½)"
33 (34.5, 37, 37) cm

1¾"
4.5 cm

20 (21½, 24½, 26½)"
51 (54.5, 62, 67.5) cm

Chain Link Pullover

෨

This cabled sweater is a surefire favorite, with the body featuring an interlocking cable-and-diamond pattern that recalls the twisted wire of a chain-link fence. The sleeves are knitted in a k2, p2 rib which ends in a cabled rib that echoes the pattern on the body. This warm woolly is a guaranteed favorite of the Young Men's/Active Casual guy. Knitted in a rich silky charcoal, it will be indispensable to the urban-styled Young Professional/Modern Casual. Choose this sweater for the following fit issues: *Average physique, Thin and/or Tall guys, Short-Waisted, Short Neck.*

SPECIFICATIONS

Finished Sizes	Yarn	Needles	Notions	Gauge
Adult S (M, L, XL). 46 (49, 52, 54½)" (117 [124.5, 132, 138.5] cm) finished chest. 25 (26, 26½, 27½)" (63.5 [66, 67.5, 70] cm) finished length. Sweater shown in size S.	Tierra Wools Organic Churro (100% wool; 800 yds [732 m]/8 oz [227g]): dark gray, 4 (4, 5, 5) skeins.	Size 9 (5.5 mm): straight or 29" (70-cm) circular (circ). Size 7 (4.5 mm): 16" (40-cm) circ. Adjust needle size if necessary to obtain the correct gauge.	Stitch markers; stitch holders; darning needle; cable needle (cn); scissors; measuring tape; crochet hook G (4.5 mm) for picking up stitches (optional).	Using larger needles, 17 sts and 23 rows = 4" (10 cm) in Stockinette st (St st) and chain link cable pattern. Check your gauge before you begin.

Back

With larger needles, loosely CO 98 (104, 110, 116) sts. Work set-up row (WS) as follows: K7 (4, 7, 4) Reverse St st (Rev St st), k4, *p4, k8; repeat from * 6 (7, 7, 8) times, p4, k4, k7 (4, 7, 4) Rev St st. On the next row (RS), work in Rev St st or Row 1 from chain link chart as follows: 7 (4, 7, 4) sts Rev St st (purl on RS, knit on WS), work Row 1 of chart over center 84 (96, 96, 108) sts, 7 (4, 7, 4) sts Rev St st. Maintaining sts at each side in Rev St st, and working center sts in chain link pat-tern from chart, work even until piece measures 14 (15, 15½, 15½)" (35.5 [38, 39.5, 39.5] cm) from begin-ning or desired length to armhole, ending with a WS row. Armhole shaping: BO 4 sts at beg of next 2 rows—90 (96, 102, 108) sts. Work even in patterns until piece measures 24 (25, 25½, 26½)" (61 [63.5, 65, 67.5] cm) from beginning, or 1" (2.5 cm) less than desired length, ending with a WS row. Shape back neck: Work 29 (31, 33, 35) sts in pattern, join new ball of yarn, BO center 32 (34, 36, 38) sts, work in pattern to end. Working

each side separately, work even in pattern until piece measures 25 (26, 26½, 27½)" (63.5 [66, 67.5, 70] cm) from beginning, or desired length. Place 29 (31, 33, 35) sts for each shoulder on separate holders.

Front

Work as for back until piece measures 21½ (22½, 23, 24)" (54.5 [57, 58.5, 61] cm) from beginning, or 3½" (9 cm) less than desired length, ending with a WS row. Shape front neck: Work 37 (39, 41, 43) sts in pattern, join new ball of yarn, BO center 16 (18, 20, 22) sts, work in pattern to end. Working each side separately, decrease 1 st at each neck edge every other row 8 times—29 (31, 33, 35) sts. Work even in pattern until piece measures 25 (26, 26½, 27½)" (63.5 [66, 67.5, 70] cm) from beginning, or desired length. Place 29 (31, 33, 35) sts for each shoulder on separate holders.

Sleeves

Matching right front and back shoulders, with right sides of fabric held together, join right shoulder using three-needle bind-off technique. Repeat for left shoulder. With RS facing, using larger needles, beginning at inner corner of armhole notch, pick up and knit 94 (94, 94, 102) sts evenly from one armhole notch to the other (using crochet hook for assistance, if desired). On the next row (WS), set up k2, p2 rib pattern as follows: *P2, k2; repeat from * to last 2 sts, end p2. Work even in rib as established until sleeve measures approximately 1" (2.5 cm) from pickup row, ending with a WS row. Shape sleeve: Beginning with the next row (RS), decrease 1 st at each side every 6 (6, 6, 4) rows 4 (4, 4, 22) times, then every 4 (4, 4, 2) rows 18 (18, 18, 4) times—50 sts for all sizes. Work even until piece measures 18½" (47 cm) from pickup row, or 2½" (6.5 cm) less than desired length, ending with a WS row. On the

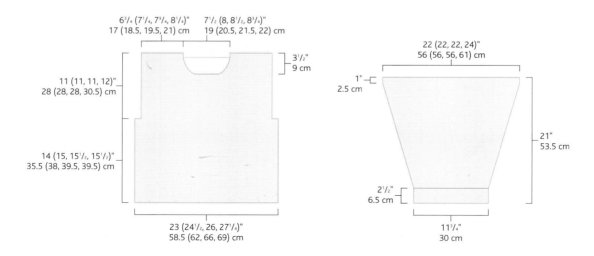

6¾ (7¼, 7¾, 8¼)"
17 (18.5, 19.5, 21) cm   7½ (8, 8½, 8¾)"
19 (20.5, 21.5, 22) cm

3½"
9 cm

11 (11, 11, 12)"
28 (28, 28, 30.5) cm

14 (15, 15½, 15½)"
35.5 (38, 39.5, 39.5) cm

23 (24½, 26, 27¼)"
58.5 (62, 66, 69) cm

22 (22, 22, 24)"
56 (56, 56, 61) cm

1"
2.5 cm

21"
53.5 cm

2½"
6.5 cm

11¾"
30 cm

next row (RS), work Row 1 of cuff cable chart to rearrange sts in preparation for working cables. Work from chart until Row 9 has been completed. Repeat Rows 2–9 *only* (do not repeat Row 1) until sleeve measures 21" (53.5 cm) from pickup row, or desired length, ending with Row 3 or Row 7, if possible. BO all sts loosely in pattern.

Finishing

Lightly steam block only if needed; blocking can compromise the rich texture of the knitting you have worked so hard to achieve. Sew straight sections at top of sleeves to armhole notches. Sew sleeve and side seams. Weave in ends.

Neckband

With smaller 16" (40-cm) circ needle, with RS facing and beginning at left shoulder seam, pick up and knit 96 (100, 104, 108) sts evenly around neck opening as follows (using crochet hook for assistance, if desired): 18 sts along side of left front neck, 20 (22, 23, 24) sts across center front, 18 sts along side of right front neck, 40 (42, 45, 48) sts across back neck. Join for working in the round (rnd), and place marker (pm) to indicate beginning of rnd. Work k2, p2 rib in the rnd for 1½" (3.8 cm), or desired length. BO all sts loosely in rib. Weave in ends.

Chain Link

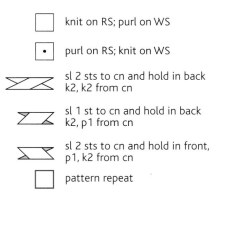

knit on RS; purl on WS

• purl on RS; knit on WS

sl 2 sts to cn and hold in back
k2, k2 from cn

sl 1 st to cn and hold in back
k2, p1 from cn

sl 2 sts to cn and hold in front,
p1, k2 from cn

pattern repeat

Cuff Cable

Cabled Rib

THE VESTS AND CARDIGANS in the Cabled Rib collection are a snap to knit and extremely versatile wardrobe pieces. Your choice of yarn can lend either an easygoing and rustic or dressy and formal feel to these up-to-date knits. For the adult version, a stiff tweed yarn makes for a sweater vest that goes perfectly with jeans or a casual pair of pants. The child's version features a drapey silk-and-cotton blend that is soft, lightweight, and perfect for a fancy occasion. The adult cardigan uses a luxurious silk-and-wool tweed, effortlessly coordinating with any outfit or situation. Great projects for a knitter new to cables, these allover cabled rib stitch garments may spend more time in *your* closet than his.

Cabled Rib Cardigan

❧

A versatile V-neck cardigan with an allover cabled rib and modern styling, this sweater features straight, clean lines without ribbing. Knitted in a lightweight silk tweed, the Cabled Rib Cardigan has a refined yet rustic quality perfect for the Young Professional/Modern Casual guy. Worked in a smooth, drapey fiber, this sweater becomes a cornerstone of the Corporate/Traditional dress-sweater collection. Choose the Cabled Rib Cardigan for the following fit issues: *Athletic and Full physiques, Short, Short-Waisted, and Round Shoulders.*

SPECIFICATIONS

Finished Sizes	Yarn	Needles	Notions	Gauge
Adult S (M, L, XL). 41 (45, 51, 55)" (104 [114.5, 129.5, 139.5] cm) finished chest. 24 (25, 26, 28)" (61 [63.5, 66, 71] cm) finished length. Cardigan shown in size L.	Garnstudio/Aurora Silke-Tweed (52% silk, 48% wool; 218 yds [200 m]/50 g): #07 green, 9 (10, 11, 12) skeins.	Size 6 (4 mm): straight or 29" (70-cm) circular (circ). Size 5 (3.75 mm): 29" (70-cm) circ. Adjust needle size if necessary to obtain the correct gauge.	Stitch markers; stitch holders; darning needle; cable needle (cn); scissors; measuring tape; five ½-inch (1.3-cm) buttons (shown: One World Button Supply, #NPL 167H Horn Barrel 15/12 mm), crochet hook F (3.75 mm) for picking up stitches (optional).	Using larger needles, 28 sts and 30 rows = 4" (10 cm) in cabled rib pattern from chart. Check your gauge before you begin.

Back

With larger straight or circ needles, CO 143 (157, 178, 192) sts. Beginning with Row 3 (cable crossing row), work Rows 3 and 4 from cabled rib pattern chart once, then repeat Rows 1–4 from chart until piece measures 13 (13½, 14, 16)" (33 [34.5, 35.5, 40.5] cm) from beginning, ending with a WS row. Armhole shaping: BO 7 sts at beg of next 2 rows— 129 (143, 164, 178) sts remain. Work even in pat-tern until piece measures 23½ (24½, 25½, 27½)" (59.5 [62, 65, 70] cm) from beginning, ending with a WS row. Shape back neck: Work 33 (40, 50, 57) sts in pattern, join new ball of yarn, BO center 63 (63, 64, 64) sts, work in pattern to end. Working each side separately, work even in pattern until piece measures 24 (25, 26, 28)" (61 [63.5, 66, 71] cm) from beginning. Place 33 (40, 50, 57) sts for each shoulder on separate holders.

Left Front

With larger straight or circ needles, CO 73 (80, 87, 94) sts. Beginning with Row 3 (cable crossing row), work Rows 3 and 4 from cabled rib pattern chart once, then repeat Rows 1–4 from chart until piece measures 13 (13½, 14, 16)" (33 [34.5, 35.5, 40.5] cm) from beginning, ending with a WS row. Shape armhole: (RS) BO 7 sts at armhole edge at beginning of row, work to end—66 (73, 80, 87) sts. Continue in pattern until piece measures 15 (15½, 16, 18)" (38 [39.5, 40.5, 45.5] cm) from beginning, ending with a WS row. Shape V neck: Beginning with the next RS row, decrease 1 st at neck edge (end of RS rows) every other row 33 (33, 30, 30) times—33 (40, 50, 57) sts rem. Work even until piece measures 24 (25, 26, 28)" (61 [63.5, 66, 71] cm) from beginning. Place sts on holder.

Right Front

Work as for left front, reversing shaping by binding off for armhole at the beginning of a WS row, and working V-neck shaping at the beginning of RS rows. Place sts on holder as for left front.

Sleeves

Matching right front and back shoulders, with right sides of fabric held together, join right shoulder using three-needle bind-off technique. Repeat for left shoulder. With RS facing, using larger needles, beginning at inner corner of armhole notch, pick up and knit 150 (157, 164, 164) sts evenly from one armhole notch to the other (using crochet hook for assistance, if desired). Beginning with WS Row 2, work Rows 2–4 from cabled rib pattern chart once, then repeat Rows 1–4 from chart until sleeve measures 1" (2.5 cm) from pickup row. Shape sleeve: Beginning with the next row, decrease 1 st at each side every 4 rows 16 (13, 8, 14) times, then every 3 rows 21 (26, 34, 26) times—76 (79, 80, 84) sts remain. Work even until sleeve measures 19 (19½, 20, 20)" (48.5 [49.5, 51, 51] cm) from pickup row, ending with Row 3 of cabled rib pattern. BO all sts.

Finishing

Lightly steam block only if needed. Sew straight sections at top of sleeves to armhole notches, sew sleeve and side seams. Weave in ends.

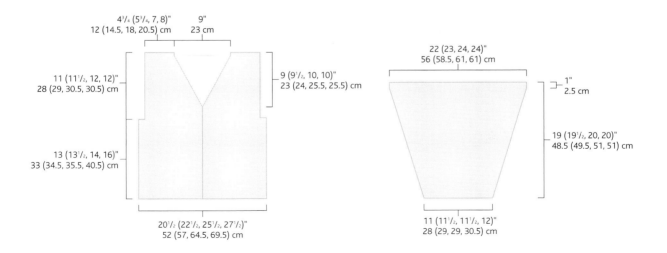

4³⁄₄ (5¹⁄₄, 7, 8)"
12 (14.5, 18, 20.5) cm

9"
23 cm

11 (11½, 12, 12)"
28 (29, 30.5, 30.5) cm

9 (9½, 10, 10)"
23 (24, 25.5, 25.5) cm

13 (13½, 14, 16)"
33 (34.5, 35.5, 40.5) cm

20½ (22½, 25½, 27½)"
52 (57, 64.5, 69.5) cm

22 (23, 24, 24)"
56 (58.5, 61, 61) cm

1"
2.5 cm

19 (19½, 20, 20)"
48.5 (49.5, 51, 51) cm

11 (11½, 11½, 12)"
28 (29, 29, 30.5) cm

Front Band

Mark positions on left front for five evenly spaced buttonholes, the lowest located ½" (1.3 cm) up from bottom edge, and the highest ½" (1.3 cm) below the beginning of the V-neck shaping. With RS facing and using smaller circ needle, beginning at bottom edge of right front, pick up and knit 286 (298, 306, 314) sts around front opening as follows (using crochet hook for assistance, if desired): 75 (78, 80, 84) sts from bottom edge to beginning of V-neck shaping, 45 (48, 50, 50) sts from beginning of V-neck shaping to shoulder seam, 46 sts along back neck, 45 (48, 50, 50) sts from left shoulder seam to beginning of V-neck shaping, 75 (78, 80, 84) sts from V-neck shaping to bottom edge. Work in k1, p1 rib, as follows for 2 rows: *K1, p1; repeat from * to end. On the next row (WS), make five 2-row buttonholes as follows: *Work in rib pattern to marked buttonhole position, BO 1 st; repeat from * 4 more times, work in rib pattern to end. On the next row (RS), CO 1 st above each gap in the buttonhole row to complete buttonholes. Work 2 more rows. BO all sts loosely in rib pattern on next row. Weave in ends. Sew buttons to right front to correspond to buttonholes.

Cabled Rib Pattern

	4
	3
	2
	1

☐ knit on RS; purl on WS

• purl on RS; knit on WS

⋉ sl 2 sts to cn and hold in back, k2, k2 from cn

☐ pattern repeat

Cabled Rib Vest—Adult

ॐ

This allover Cabled Rib Vest is extremely versatile, with straight, clean lines and no ribbing. A rustic, rich tweed yarn dresses down the vest to make it a perfect complement to jeans. If knitted in a drapey, smooth yarn, the vest can accompany a tie for just about any dressy occasion. This vest fits the wardrobe of all Personal Style categories. Choose it for the following fit issues: *Athletic and Full physiques, Short, and any physical attribute that is enhanced by a V neck.*

SPECIFICATIONS

Finished Sizes	Yarn	Needles	Notions	Gauge
Adult S (M, L, XL). 41 (45, 51, 55)" (104 [114.5, 129.5, 139.5] cm) finished chest. 24 (24, 25, 27)" (61 [61, 63.5, 68.5] cm) finished length. Vest shown in size M.	Black Water Abbey Two-Ply (100% wool; 220 yds [200 m]/4 oz [114 g]): bluestack, 5 (5, 6, 7) skeins.	Size 6 (4 mm): straight or 29" (70-cm) circular (circ). Size 5 (3.75 mm): 16" (40-cm) and 29" (70-cm) circ. Adjust needle size if necessary to obtain the correct gauge.	Stitch markers; stitch holders; darning needle; cable needle (cn); scissors; measuring tape; five ⅝-inch (1.6-cm) buttons (shown: One World Button Supply, #SPN 105-28HK Bubble Tagua Huckleberry 28 mm), crochet hook F (4 mm) for picking up stitches (optional).	Using larger needles, 28 sts and 30 rows = 4" (10 cm) in cabled rib pattern from chart. Check your gauge before you begin.

Back

With larger straight or circ needles, CO 143 (157, 178, 192) sts. Beginning with Row 3 (cable crossing row), work Rows 3 and 4 from cabled rib pattern chart once, then repeat Rows 1–4 from chart until piece measures 13 (13, 13½, 15)" (33 [33, 34.5, 38] cm) from beginning, ending with a WS row. Armhole shaping: BO 12 sts at beg of next 2 rows—119 (133, 154, 168) sts remain. Beginning with the next RS row, dec 1 st each at each side every other row 11 times—97 (111, 132, 146) sts. Work even in pattern until piece measures 23½ (23½, 24½, 26½)" (59.5 [59.5, 62, 67.5] cm) from beginning, ending with a WS row. Shape back neck: Work 24 (29, 38, 43) sts in

pattern, join new ball of yarn, BO center 49 (53, 56, 60) sts, work in pattern to end. Working each side separately, work even in pattern until piece measures 24 (24, 25, 27)" (61 [61, 63.5, 68.5] cm) from beginning. Place 24 (29, 38, 43) sts for each shoulder on separate holders.

Left Front

With larger straight or circ needles, CO 73 (80, 87, 94) sts. Beginning with Row 3 (cable crossing row), work Rows 3 and 4 from cabled rib pattern chart once, then repeat Rows 1–4 from chart until piece measures 13 (13, 13½, 15)" (33 [33, 34.5, 38] cm) from beginning, ending with a WS row. Shape armhole and V neck: (RS) BO 12

sts at armhole edge at beginning of row, work to end—61 (68, 75, 82) sts. Beginning with the next RS row, dec 1 st at armhole edge every other row 11 times, and *at the same time,* when piece measures 14 (14, 15, 17)" (35.5 [35.5, 38, 43] cm) from beginning, shape V neck by dec 1 st at neck edge every other row 6 (12, 6, 12) times, then every 3 rows 20 (16, 20, 16) times—24 (29, 38, 43) sts remain. Work even if necessary until piece measures 24 (24, 25, 27)" (61 [61, 63.5, 68.5] cm) from beginning. Place sts on holder.

Right Front

Work as for left front, reversing shaping by binding off for armhole at the beginning of a WS row, and working V-neck shaping at the beginning of RS rows or the end of WS rows. Place sts on holder as for left front.

Finishing

Matching right front and back shoulders, with right sides facing, join right shoulder using three-needle bind-off technique. Repeat for left shoulder. Lightly steam block only if needed. Sew side seams. Weave in ends.

Front Band

Mark positions on left front for five evenly spaced buttonholes, the lowest located ½" (1.3 cm) up from bottom edge, and the highest ½" (1.3 cm) below the beginning of the V-neck shaping. With RS facing and using longer length smaller circ needle, beginning at bottom edge of right front, pick up and knit 231 (235, 243, 259) sts around front opening as follows (using crochet hook for assistance, if desired): 53 (53, 55, 61) sts from bottom edge to beginning of V-neck shaping, 40 sts from beginning of V-neck shaping to shoulder seam, 45 (49, 53, 57) sts along back neck, 40 sts from left shoulder seam to beginning of V-neck shaping, 53 (53, 55, 61) sts from V-neck shaping to bottom edge. Establish k1, p1 rib as follows: (WS) *P1, k1; repeat from *, end p1. Work 1 row even in k1, p1 rib (work all sts as they appear). On the next row (WS), make five 2-row buttonholes as follows: *Work in rib pattern to marked buttonhole position, BO 2 sts; repeat from * 4 more times, work in rib pattern to end. On the next row (RS), CO 2 sts above each gap in the buttonhole row to complete buttonholes. Work 3 more rows. BO all sts loosely in rib pattern on next row. Weave in ends. Sew buttons to right front to correspond to buttonholes.

Armhole Finishing

With RS facing and using smaller size 16" (40-cm) circ needle, beginning at underarm seam, pick up and knit 118 (118, 122, 128) sts evenly around armhole edge, (using crochet hook for assistance, if desired). Join for working in the round (rnd) and work in k1, p1 rib for 1 rnd. BO all sts loosely in rib on next rnd. Weave in ends. Repeat for other armhole.

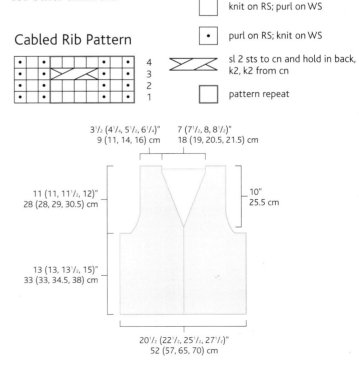

Cabled Rib Pattern

knit on RS; purl on WS

· purl on RS; knit on WS

sl 2 sts to cn and hold in back, k2, k2 from cn

pattern repeat

3½ (4¼, 5½, 6¼)"
9 (11, 14, 16) cm

7 (7½, 8, 8½)"
18 (19, 20.5, 21.5) cm

11 (11, 11½, 12)"
28 (28, 29, 30.5) cm

10"
25.5 cm

13 (13, 13½, 15)"
33 (33, 34.5, 38) cm

20½ (22½, 25½, 27½)"
52 (57, 65, 70) cm

Cabled Rib Vest—Child

A slightly dressy vest for a dapper young man. The pipsqueak of the Cabled Rib group, this adorable vest is knitted in an easy-care cotton blended with silk and rayon. The kids' version features a hemmed stockinette stitch buttonband, and like the big boys' version, clean straight lines and no ribbing.

SPECIFICATIONS

Finished Sizes	Yarn	Needles	Notions	Gauge
Child S (M, L), to fit 4 (6/8, 10/12) years. 31 (33, 35)" (78.5 [84, 89] cm) finished chest. 15 (16, 18)" (38 [40.5, 45.5] cm) finished length. Vest shown in size S, to fit 4 years.	Dale of Norway Svale (50% cotton, 40% viscose, 10% silk; 114 yds [104 m]/50 g): #9451 moss green, 6 (7, 8) skeins.	Size 7 (4.5 mm): straight. Size 5 (3.75 mm): 29" (70-cm) circular (circ) and 16" (40-cm) circ. Adjust needle size if necessary to obtain the correct gauge.	Stitch markers; stitch holders; darning needle; cable needle (cn); scissors; measuring tape; five 1/2-inch (1.3-cm) buttons (shown: Blue Moon Buttons, Coconut Shell Q1012), crochet hook G (4.5 mm) for picking up stitches (optional).	Using larger needles, 28 sts and 30 rows = 4" (10 cm) in cabled rib pattern from chart. Check your gauge before you begin.

Back

With larger needles, CO 108 (115, 122) sts. Work even in cabled rib pattern from chart until piece measures 8 (9, 10½)" (20.5 [23, 26.5] cm) or desired length to underarm ending with a WS row. Armhole shaping: BO 7 sts at beg of next 2 rows—94 (101, 108) sts remain. Beginning with the next RS row, dec 1 st each at each side every other row 10 (9, 7) times—74 (83, 94) sts. Work even in pattern until piece measures 15 (16, 18)" (38 [40.5, 45.5] cm) from beginning, ending with a WS row. Shape back neck: Work 18 (20, 23) sts in pattern, BO center 38 (43, 48) sts, work in pattern to end. Place 18 (20, 23) sts for each shoulder on separate holders.

Left Front

With larger needles, CO 52 (59, 59) sts. Work even in cabled rib pattern from chart until piece measures 8 (9, 10½)" (20.5 [23, 26.5] cm) or desired length to underarm ending with a WS row. Shape armhole and V neck: (RS) BO 7 sts at armhole edge at beginning of row, work to last 3 sts, work 2 sts together in pattern, work last st— 44 (51, 51) sts. Continue in pattern, and at the same time, dec 1 st at armhole edge every other row 9 (8, 6) more times, and decrease 1 st at V-neck edge as before every other row 17 (23, 22) times—18 (20, 23) sts rem. Work even until piece measures 15 (16, 18)" (38 [40.5, 45.5] cm) from beginning. Place sts on holder.

Right Front

Work as for left front, reversing shaping by beginning armhole and V-neck shaping on a WS row. Place sts on holder as for left front.

Finishing

Matching right front and back shoulders, with right sides facing, join right shoulder using three-needle bind-off technique. Repeat for left shoulder. Lightly steam block only if needed. Sew side seams. Weave in ends.

Front Band

Mark positions on left front for five evenly spaced buttonholes, the lowest located ½" (1.3 cm) up from bottom edge, and the highest ½" (1.3 cm) below the beginning of the V-neck shaping. With RS facing and using 29" (70-cm) smaller circ needle, beg at bottom edge of right front, pick up and knit 225 (240, 270) sts around front opening as follows (using crochet hook for assistance, if desired): 54 (60, 70) sts from bottom edge to beginning of V-neck shaping, 41 (41, 44) sts from beginning of V-neck shaping to shoulder seam, 35 (38, 42) sts along back neck, 41 (41, 44) sts from left shoulder seam to beginning of V-neck shaping, 54 (60, 70) sts from V-neck shaping to bottom edge. Work in Stockinette stitch (St st) for 2 rows, beginning with a WS row. On the next row (WS), make five 2-row buttonholes as follows: *Purl to marked buttonhole position, BO 1 st; repeat from * 4 more times, purl to end. On the next row (RS), CO 1 st above each gap in the buttonhole row to complete buttonholes. Work 2 more rows. Knit 1 row on WS for facing turning ridge. Knit 1 row on RS. On the next row (WS), make five 2-row buttonholes in the same manner

as given above. On the next row (RS), CO 1 st above each gap in the buttonhole row to complete buttonholes. Work 2 more rows St st. BO all sts loosely. Fold front band along turning ridge and slip-stitch band in place on wrong side. Join two layers of each buttonhole by working buttonhole st around each hole through both layers of band. Weave in ends. Sew buttons to right front to correspond to buttonholes.

Armhole Finishing

With RS facing and using shorter circ needle, beginning at underarm seam, pick up and knit 105 (105, 112) sts evenly around armhole edge, (using crochet hook for assistance, if desired). Join for working in the round and loosely BO all sts as if to knit on next round. Weave in ends. Repeat for other armhole.

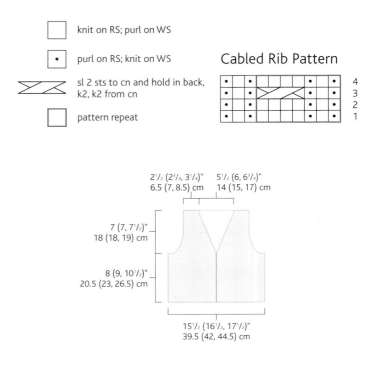

knit on RS; purl on WS

• purl on RS; knit on WS

sl 2 sts to cn and hold in back, k2, k2 from cn

pattern repeat

Cabled Rib Pattern

2½ (2¾, 3¼)"
6.5 (7, 8.5) cm

5½ (6, 6¾)"
14 (15, 17) cm

7 (7, 7½)"
18 (18, 19) cm

8 (9, 10½)"
20.5 (23, 26.5) cm

15½ (16½, 17½)"
39.5 (42, 44.5) cm

Perpendicular Lines Pullover

A traditional style with playful updates, this V neck is a fun introduction to color knitting. With its horizontal color borders and vertical seeded rib, the Perpendicular Lines Pullover juxtaposes texture and color while remaining understated. The body of the sweater is knitted in the round, and the sleeves are knitted back and forth. This pattern best suits fellows in the Young Professional/Modern Casual and Corporate/Traditional Personal Styles. It is a good choice for the following fit issues: *Athletic or Average physique, Tall, Wide Chest, and Long Torso.*

SPECIFICATIONS

Finished Sizes	Yarn	Needles	Notions	Gauge
Adult S (M, L, XL). 40 (44½, 49, 53)" (101.5 [113, 124.5, 134.5] cm) finished chest. 24 (25, 26, 27)" (61 [63.5, 66, 68.5] cm) finished length. Sweater shown in size M.	Mission Falls 1824 Wool (100% machine-washable Merino wool; 84 yds [77 m]/50 g): #005 raven (black), 12 (13, 15, 16) skeins; #016 thyme (green), 1 (1, 2, 2) skeins; #013 curry (gold), #003 oyster (gray), #004 charcoal, and #021 denim, 1 skein each.	Size 8 (5 mm): 29" (70-cm) circular (circ). Size 6 (4 mm): 29" (70-cm) and 16" (40-cm) circ. Adjust needle size if necessary to obtain the correct gauge.	Stitch markers; stitch holders; darning needle; scissors; measuring tape; crochet hook H (5 mm) for picking up stitches (optional).	Using larger needles, 18 sts and 24 rows = 4" (10 cm) in Stockinette stitch (St st). Check your gauge before you begin.

Wide Seed Stitch Rib in the Round (multiple of 10 sts)

Rnd 1: K5, p1, *k9, p1; repeat from * to last 4 sts, end k4.

Rnd 2: K4, p1, k1, *k8, p1, k1; repeat from * to last 4 sts, end k4.

Repeat these 2 rnds for pattern.

Wide Seed Stitch Rib in Rows (multiple of 10 sts)

Row 1: (WS) P4, *k1, p9; repeat from * to last 6 sts, end k1, p5.

Row 2: K4, p1, k1, *k8, p1, k1; repeat from * to last 4 sts, end k4.

Repeat these 2 rows for pattern.

Body

With smaller needle and black, CO 172 (192, 210, 230) sts. Join, being careful not to twist, and place marker (pm) to indicate beginning of round (rnd). Work in k1, p1 rib for 2" (5 cm), increasing 8 (8, 10, 10) sts

evenly in last rnd—180 (200, 220, 240) sts. Change to larger needles and work Rows 1–21 of colorwork chart in St st the rnd, beginning and ending where indicated for body, and adding new colors as needed. When colorwork chart has been completed, change to wide seed st rib in the rnd, and work even with black until piece measures 14 (14, 14½, 15)" (35.5 [35.5, 37, 38] cm) from beginning. On the next rnd, divide for front and back as follows: BO 9 (10, 11, 12) sts, work 72 (80, 88, 96) sts as established, BO 18 (20, 22, 24) sts, work 72 (80, 88, 96) sts as established, BO 9 (10, 11, 12) sts. The group of sts to be worked next are the sts for the back.

Back

Leaving sts for front unworked on the cable part of the circ needle, continue established wide seed st rib on back sts, working back and forth in rows as follows: maintain 8-st columns of St st, separated by 2-st columns of seed st (knit the purls, and purl the knits as they appear). Work in pattern until back measures 23¼ (24¼, 25¼, 26¼)" (59 [61.5, 64, 66.5] cm) from beginning, ending with a WS row. Shape back neck: (RS) Work 20 (24, 27, 30) sts, join second ball of yarn, BO center 32 (32, 34, 36) sts, work

to end. Working each side separately, work even until piece measures 24 (25, 26, 27)" (61 [63.5, 66, 68.5] cm) from beginning. Place 20 (24, 27, 30) sts for each shoulder on separate holders.

Front

Join black to sts on cable needle for front with RS facing—72 (80, 88, 96) sts. Work as for back until piece measures 16½ (17½, 18, 19)" (42 [44.5, 45.5, 48.5] cm) from beginning, ending with a WS row. Shape V neck: (RS) Work 36 (40, 44, 48) sts, join second ball of yarn, work 36 (40, 44, 48) sts to end. Working each side separately, decrease 1 st at each neck edge every other row 6 (6, 6, 9) times, then every 3 rows 10 (10, 11, 9) times—20 (24, 27, 30) sts. Work even until piece measures 24 (25, 26, 27)" (61 [63.5, 66, 68.5] cm) from beginning. Place 20 (24, 27, 30) sts for each shoulder on separate holders.

Sleeves

Matching right front and back shoulders, with right sides of fabric held together and using black, join right shoulder using three-needle bind-off technique. Repeat for left shoulder. With RS facing, using larger needles and

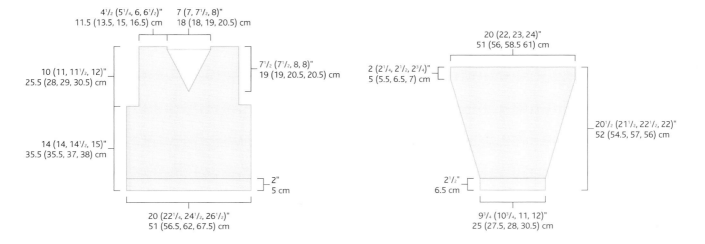

4½ (5¼, 6, 6½)"
11.5 (13.5, 15, 16.5) cm

7 (7, 7½, 8)"
18 (18, 19, 20.5) cm

10 (11, 11½, 12)"
25.5 (28, 29, 30.5) cm

7½ (7½, 8, 8)"
19 (19, 20.5, 20.5) cm

14 (14, 14½, 15)"
35.5 (35.5, 37, 38) cm

2"
5 cm

20 (22¼, 24½, 26½)"
51 (56.5, 62, 67.5) cm

20 (22, 23, 24)"
51 (56, 58.5 61) cm

2 (2¼, 2½, 2¾)"
5 (5.5, 6.5, 7) cm

20½ (21½, 22½, 22)"
52 (54.5, 57, 56) cm

2½"
6.5 cm

9¾ (10¾, 11, 12)"
25 (27.5, 28, 30.5) cm

black, beginning at inner corner of armhole notch, pick up and knit 90 (98, 104, 108) sts evenly from one armhole notch to the other (using crochet hook for assistance, if desired). On the next row (WS), establish wide seed st rib as follows: P0 (4, 2, 4), work wide seed rib in rows over center 90 (90, 100, 100) sts, p0 (4, 2, 4). Maintaining sts at each side of pattern in St st, work even until sleeve measures 2 (2¼, 2½, 2¾)" (5 [5.5, 6.5, 7] cm) from pickup row. Shape sleeve: Continue in pattern, and beginning with the next RS row, decrease 1 st at each side every 4 rows 15 (14, 15, 10) times, then every 3 rows 4 (7, 7, 12) times—52 (56, 60, 64) sts. Work even until piece measures 14½ (15½, 16½, 16)" (35.5 [39.5, 42, 40.5] cm) from pickup row, or 6" (15 cm) less than desired

Perpendicular Lines Colorwork Chart

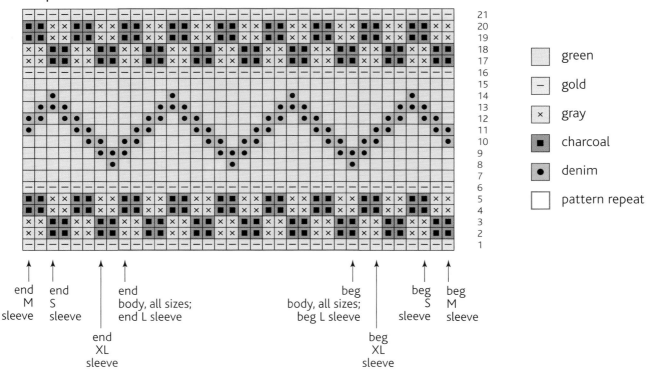

length, ending with a WS row. Work Rows 1–21 of colorwork chart in St st, beginning and ending where indicated for your size, and adding new colors as needed. When colorwork chart has been completed, change to black and purl one row, dec 8 (8, 10, 10) sts evenly across—44 (48, 50, 54) sts. Change to smaller needles, and work in k1, p1 rib with black for 2½" (6.5 cm). BO all sts loosely in rib.

Finishing

Lightly steam block only if needed; blocking can compromise the rich texture of the knitting you have worked so hard to achieve. Sew straight sections at top of sleeves to BO sections of armhole notches. Sew sleeve seams. Weave in ends.

Neckband

With smaller 16" (40-cm) circ needle and black, with RS facing and beginning at left shoulder seam, pick up and knit 113 (113, 119, 123) sts around neck opening as follows (using crochet hook for assistance, if desired): 38 (38, 40, 40) sts along left side neck, pm, 1 st from base of V-neck shaping, pm, 38 (38, 40, 40) sts along right side neck, 36 (36, 38, 42) sts across back neck. Join for working in the rnd. Next rnd: Work in k1, p1 rib to 2 sts before first marker, ssk, slip marker (sl m), k1 (center st), sl m, k2tog, work in k1, p1 rib to end—111 (111, 117, 121) sts. Work 5 more rnds in this manner, decreasing on either side of center marked st on each rnd—101 (101, 107, 111) sts. BO all sts loosely in rib pattern. Weave in ends.

Tweeds Cardigan, with Scarf

A rich, thick tweedy yarn combined with a textured "tweed" stitch lends this relaxed V-neck cardigan a warm, jacketlike quality. Worn casually with pants, it suits the Young Men's/Active Casual style; worn with a shirt and tie, it's a perfect jacket for the Young Professional/Modern Casual guy. The slip-stitch pattern and big gauge make for an easy-to-knit and easy-going sweater. Consider this pattern for the following fit issues: *All physiques, Wide Chest, Short-Waisted, Short Arms, Short Neck.*

SPECIFICATIONS

Finished Sizes	Yarn	Needles	Notions	Gauge
Adult S (M, L, XL). 42 (44½, 50, 54)" (106.5 [113, 127, 137] cm) finished chest. 24 (25, 26, 27)" (61 [63.5, 66, 68.5] cm) finished length. Cardigan shown in size M. Scarf measures approximately 7" x 45" (18 x 114.5 cm).	Naturally/S. R. Kertzer Natural Wool Chunky 14-ply (100% wool; 244 yds [225 m]/200 g): #921 light brown (MC), 5 (5, 6, 6) skeins; #923 dark brown (CC), 1 skein for cardigan; approximately 150 yds (137 m) CC, and 15 yds (13.5 m) MC for scarf.	Size 10½ (6.5 mm): straight or 29" (70-cm) circular (circ). Size 9 (5.5 mm): 29" (70-cm) circ. Adjust needle size if necessary to obtain the correct gauge.	Stitch markers; stitch holders; darning needle; scissors; measuring tape; five ⁷⁄₈-inch (2.2-cm) buttons (shown: One World Button Supply, SPN 105-36HK Bubble Tagua Huckleberry 36L), crochet hook K (6.5 mm) for picking up stitches (optional).	Using larger needles, 14 sts and 17 rows = 4" (10 cm) in tweed stitch pattern. Check your gauge before you begin.

Tweed Stitch (even number of stitches)

Row 1: (RS) K1, *k1, sl 1 pwise wyif (slip 1 as if to purl with yarn in front); repeat from * to last st, end k1.

Rows 2 and 4: Purl all sts.

Row 3: K1, *sl 1 pwise wyif, k1; repeat from * to last st, end k1.

Repeat these 4 rows for pattern.

Back

With larger needles, loosely CO 74 (78, 88, 94) sts. Work in tweed st until piece measures 12½ (13, 13½, 14)" (32 [33, 34.5, 35.5] cm) from beginning, or 1" (2.5 cm) less than desired length to underarm, ending with a WS row. Armhole shaping: BO 3 sts at beg of next 2 rows—68 (72, 82, 88) sts remain. Work even in pattern until piece measures 23½ (24½, 25½, 26½)" (59.5 [62, 65, 67.5] cm) from beginning, ending with a WS row. Shape back neck: Work 22 (23, 26, 28) sts in pattern, join new ball of yarn, BO center 24 (26, 30, 32) sts, work in pattern to end. Working each side separately, work even in pattern until piece measures 24 (25, 26, 27)" (61 [63.5, 66, 68.5] cm) from begin-

ning. Place 22 (23, 26, 28) sts for each shoulder on separate holders.

Left Front

With larger needles, loosely CO 36 (38, 44, 46) sts. Work in tweed st until piece measures 12½ (13, 13½, 14)" (32 [33, 34.5, 35.5] cm) from beginning, or 1" (2.5 cm) less than desired length to underarm, ending with a WS row. Armhole shaping: BO 3 sts at beg of next row—33 (35, 41, 43) sts remain. Work even in pattern until piece measures 2" (5 cm) above armhole shaping, ending with a WS row. Shape V neck: Beginning on the next RS row, decrease 1 st at neck edge (end of RS rows, beginning of WS rows) every 2 rows 0 (0, 7, 5) times, then every 3 rows 11 (12, 8, 10) times—22 (23, 26, 28) sts. Work even in pattern until piece measures 24 (25, 26, 27)" (61 [63.5, 66, 68.5] cm) from beginning. Place 22 (23, 26, 28) sts on holder.

Right Front

Work as for left front, reversing shaping by binding off for armhole at the beginning of a WS row, and working V-neck shaping at the beginning of RS rows or end of WS rows. Place sts on holder as for left front.

Sleeves

Matching right front and back shoulders, with right sides of fabric held together, join right shoulder using three-needle bind-off technique. Repeat for left shoulder. With RS facing and using larger needles, beginning at inner corner of armhole notch, pick up and knit 74 (78, 82, 84) sts evenly from one armhole notch to the other (using crochet hook for assistance, if desired). Work in tweed st pattern until sleeve measures 1" (2.5 cm) from pickup row, ending with a WS row. Shape sleeve: Beginning with the next RS row, decrease 1 st at each side every 5 rows 5 (4, 6, 3) times, then every 3 rows 13 (15, 14, 18) times—38 (40, 42, 42) sts remain. Work even until sleeve measures 16 (16½, 17½, 17½)" (40.5 [42, 44.5, 44.5] cm) from pickup row, or 2½" (6.5 cm) less than desired length. Change to smaller circ needle and work in k1, p1 rib for 1½" (3.8 cm), ending with a WS row. Change to CC and work in St st for 6 rows. BO all sts loosely.

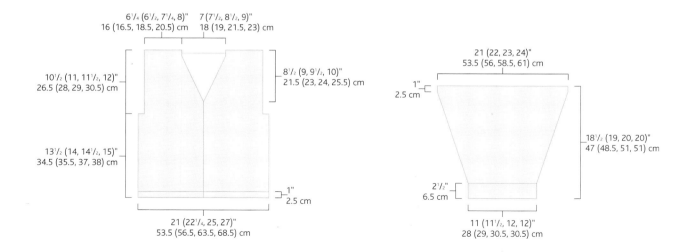

Finishing

Lightly steam block only if needed; blocking can compromise the rich texture of the knitting you have worked so hard to achieve. Sew sleeve and side seams, reversing the seam for the rolled edges of sleeves so RS of seams will show when purl side of St st sections rolls to the outside of garment. Weave in ends.

Front Band and Lower Edge

Mark positions on left front for five evenly spaced buttonholes, the lowest located ½" (1.3 cm) up from bottom edge, and the highest ½" (1.3 cm) below the beginning of the V-neck shaping. With RS facing, using smaller circ needle and MC, beginning at bottom edge of right front, pick up and knit 236 (246, 258, 268) sts around front opening as follows (using crochet hook for assistance, if desired): 62 (64, 66, 68) sts from bottom edge to beginning of V-neck shaping, 39 (41, 43, 45) sts from beginning of V-neck shaping to shoulder seam, 34 (36, 40, 42) sts along back neck, 39 (41, 43, 45) sts from left shoulder seam to beginning of V-neck shaping, 62 (64, 66, 68) sts from V-neck shaping to bottom edge. Work in k1, p1 rib, for 1 row. On the next row (RS), make five 2-row buttonholes as follows: *Work in rib pattern to marked buttonhole position, BO 2 sts; repeat from * 4 more times, work in rib pattern to end. On the next row (WS), CO 2 sts above each gap in the buttonhole row to complete buttonholes. Work 2 more rows. On the next row (RS), change to CC and BO all sts loosely as if to knit, but do not cut yarn. With RS facing and using same needle, pick up and knit 146 (155, 174, 188) sts evenly around lower edge as follows (using crochet hook for assistance, if desired): 37 (39, 44, 47) sts from center front to side seam, 72 (77, 86, 94) sts across back, 37 (39, 44, 47) sts from side seam to center front. Work in St st for 7 rows. BO all sts loosely; rolled edge will roll up to about 1" (2.5 cm) high. Weave in ends. Sew buttons to right front to correspond to buttonholes.

Scarf

Using larger needles and MC, CO 24 sts loosely. Work in St st for 6 rows or desired length for contrasting edge. Change to CC and work in tweed st until piece measures 43¼" (110 cm) or 1¾" (4.5 cm) less than desired length, ending with a RS row. Change to MC and, beginning with a purl row, work in St st for 6 rows or same length as other contrasting edge. BO all sts loosely. Weave in ends. Block lightly, if desired.

Terms and Abbreviations

Beg	Beginning
BO	Bind off
CO	Cast on
Cont	Continue
CN	Cable needle
Dec	Decrease
DPN	Double-pointed needle(s)
EOR	Every other row
Foll	Following or follows
Gauge	The number of stitches and rows equal to a given measurement. Achieving the specified gauge is essential to ensure correct sizing when you are knitting from a pattern.
In	Inch
Inc	Increase
K	Knit
K2tog	Knit two stitches together to decrease to 1 stitch
LHN	Left-hand needle
Meas	Measures
P	Purl
Patt	Pattern
PM	Place marker
PSSO	Pass the slipped stitch over
Rem	Remaining or remains
Rep	Repeat
RHN	Right-hand needle
Rnd	Round
RS	Right side, usually the "public" side of the knitting
SL	Slip
SPN	Single-pointed needle
SSK	Slip, slip, knit—slip 2 sts one at a time as if to knit, insert LHN into back of both sts, k2tog through their back loops to decrease to 1 stitch
St st	Stockinette or stocking stitch
St(s)	Stitch(es)
Tog	Together
WS	Wrong side,
WYIF	With yarn in front

Techniques

Picking Up Stitches with the Aid of a Crochet Hook

Using this method for sleeves gives great results—a perfect shoulder join with what appears to be a magnificent seam, and two less seams to sew! Indeed it's a great technique for those who don't count finishing among their favorite things to do on a Saturday night.

Set Up: With RS facing, hold a crochet hook in your dominant hand and a new strand of yarn behind the work. Make sure you are picking up sts with the working end of the yarn connected to the ball, not the tail. Choose a straight column of sts in which to pick up your new sts. It should be easy to see, yet as close to your selvedge edge as possible, say, between the first and second sts of each row. Whatever column you choose, be very careful to pick up sts consistently along the same line. If the line of picked-up sts wavers, you will not achieve a perfectly neat and even join.

Picking up Stitches: Insert the crochet hook at your chosen place and catch the yarn held behind the work. Pull a new loop through to the RS. Place the loop on a free knitting needle and pull snugly to match the tension of your knitting. Rep as many times as needed. A good rate tends to be about 3 sts picked up for every 4 rows of knitting, but you should use your gauge and the pattern as a guide to how many sts to pick up per inch.

Three-Needle Bind-Off Technique

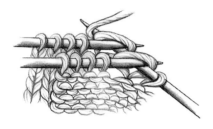

As the name suggests, three needles are needed for this process. You may also use both ends of a circular needle, plus one additional straight needle. BO shoulder sts together as follows: Carefully matching the shoulders left to left, or right to right, place sts from holders onto two needles so that right sides of each piece are touching and the needle tips point in same direction. Holding needles parallel, insert the third needle into the first 2 sts on each of the other needles, and knit them together. *Knit the next 2 sts together in the same manner; there will be 2 sts on the right needle. Pass the first st on the right needle over the second, as if to BO; rep from * until all sts are bound off. Cut yarn, leaving a 6–10" tail, draw tail through the remaining st. Repeat for other shoulder.

Two-Row Buttonhole

Work the number of rows specified before the buttonhole. Buttonhole Row 1: Work in patt to location of first buttonhole, BO 2 sts, *continue in patt to location of next buttonhole, BO 2 sts, repeat from * until all buttonholes

have been completed, work in patt to end. Buttonhole Row 2: *Work in patt to gap formed by bound-off sts of previous row, CO 2 sts over the gap; rep from * until all buttonholes have been completed, work in patt to end.

Stitching the Sleeve Extension into the Armhole Notch

This step will be necessary for garments with modified dropped shoulder armholes. To complete armhole before sewing the side seams, invisibly sew the sides of each sleeve extension to the notches created when you bound off sts for the armhole.

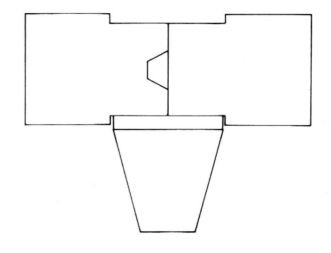

Recommended Increase Method

Make 1 (M1): Insert right needle under the strand between the two needles from back to front and place this strand on the left needle. Knit this new loop through the back, twisting the st to avoid making making a hole.

Figure 1   *Figure 2*

Sources and Further Reading

Donohue, Amy. "Perfectly Fit," *Men's Health,* December 2000, Vol. 15, Issue 10.

Jackson, Carole. *Color for Men.* New York: Ballantine Books, 1987.

Kirkpatrick, John. "Men's Clothing Industry Gears Up for Resurgence," *Dallas Morning News,* February 16, 2002.

Mountford, Debra (ed). *The Harmony Guide to Aran and Fair Isle Knitting,* New York: Crown Publishing, 1995.

Newton, Deborah. *Designing Knitwear,* Newtown, Connecticut: Taunton Press, 1998.

O'Neill, Hugh. "Knits Worth Picking," *Men's Health,* November 2000, Vol. 15, Issue 9.

Reader's Digest Association. *Reader's Digest Complete Book of Sewing,* Pleasantville, New York: Reader's Digest Association, 1997.

Revelli, Clare. *Color and You,* New York: Pocket Books, 1989.

Sewing for Men and Boys, New York: Simplicity Pattern Company, 1973.

Vogue Knitting: The Ultimate Knitting Book, New York: Soho Publishing Company, 2002.

"What to Wear to Work," *Esquire,* October 2000, Vol. 134, Issue 4.

White, Jackie. "In These Uncertain Times, Menswear Can Count on Mix and Match Classics," *Kansas City Star,* August 1, 2001.

White, Renee Minus. "Fall 2001 Menswar," *New York Amsterdam News,* May 31, 2001, Vol. 92, Issue 22.

Resources

Yarn kits for projects in this book and Tara Jon Manning's original design patterns are available from

Tara Handknitting Designs, PO Box 573, Boulder, CO 80304-0573, www.tarahandknitting.com.

Materials featured in this book have been supplied by:

Black Water Abbey Yarns, PO Box 470688, Aurora, CO 80047-0688, (720) 320-1003, www.abbeyyarns.com.

Cascade Yarn, Inc., 1224 Andover Park E., Tukwila, WA 98188, www.cascadeyarns.com.

Classic Elite Yarns, 300 Jackson St., Lowell, MA 01852, (800) 343-0308.

Crystal Palace Yarns, 2320 Bissell Ave., Richmond, CA 94804, (510) 237-9988, www.straw.com.

Dale of Norway, N16 W23390 Stoneridge Dr., Ste. A, Waukesha, WI 53188, (800) 441-DALE, www.dale.no.

Joseph Galler Yarns, 5 Mercury Ave., Monroe, NY 10950, (800) 836-3314.

Garnstudio/Aurora Yarns, PO Box 3068, Moss Beach, CA 94038, (650) 728-2730, www.garnstudio.com.

Horstia/Muench Yarns, 285 Bel Marin Keys Blvd., Unit J, Novato, CA 94949-5763, (415) 883-6375, www.muenchyarns.com.

Mission Falls, Distributed in the United States by Unique Kolours, 1428 Oak Ln., Downingtown, PA 19335, (800) 25-2DYE4, www.missionfalls.com.

Naturally/SR Kertzer, 105a Winges Rd., Woodbridge, ON, Canada L4L 6C2, (800) 263-2354, www.kertzer.com.

One World Button Supply Company, 41 Union Square West, Ste. 311, New York, NY 10003, (212) 691-1331. One World Button Supply Co. was founded in 1995

to market handcrafted buttons from micro-enterprise development programs of nonprofit and nongovernmental organizations. One World's artisans rely on natural sustainable resources at hand, technical skills passed from generation to generation, and designs rich in cultural reference. They work in their own communities to elevate workers' conditions and protect the environment. By supporting One World you support women's cooperatives, rural development programs, and workshops for the disabled, and you further the growth of those organizations into independent, self-supporting enterprises. All of One World's resources adhere to the principles of Fair Trade. For more information on Fair Trade, visit www.maketradefair.com, www.transfairusa.org, www.datadata.org/abouttrade.htm.

Plymouth Yarn Company, Inc., PO Box 28, Bristol, PA 19007, (800) 523-8932, www.plymouthyarn.com.

Reynolds Yarn/JCA, Inc., 35 Scales Ln., Townsend, MA 01469, (800) 225-6340, www.jcacrafts.com.

Rowan Yarns, Rowan USA, 4 Townsend West, Ste. 8, Nashua, NH 03063, (603) 886-5041, www.knitrowan.com.

Tierra Wools, Los Ojos Handweavers, LLC, 91 Main St., PO Box 229, Los Ojos, NM 87551, (888) 709-0979, www.organicyarn.com.

Tierra Wools is a community-based nonprofit organization with the mission of empowering rural people to create sustainable economies by building on cultural and agricultural resources in New Mexico's Chama Valley. The organization is one of only a few suppliers of organically raised yarn and wool in the United States, and to preserve the organic qualities of the wool, their yarns are washed and woolen spun without spinning oil and dyed with all-natural dyes using alum/cream of tartar mordants. In this way, Tierra Wools furthers the tradition of natural dyeing with plants from the wild and exotic natural dyestuffs, as practiced for hundreds of years by the region's Spanish settlers and the Hopi, Navajo, and Pueblo tribes. The yarn shown in the Chain Link Pullover is made from the wool of the churro, a breed of sheep brought to the New World by the Spanish in the 1500s. For more information on U.S. Organic standards, production, and products visit The National Organic Program, www.ams.usda.gov/nop; The Organic Trade Association, www.ota.com.

No-rinse woolwash for laundering natural fibers and handknitted garments:

Eucalan, PO Box 374, Paris, ON, Canada N3L 3T5, (800) 561-9731, www.eucalan.com.

Menswear Websites

www.bananarepublic.com

www.dolcegabbana.it

www.giorgioarmani.com

www.guess.com

www.helmutlang.com

www.hugoboss.com

www.jcrew.com

www.kennethcole.com

www.polo.com

www.tommy.com

www.versace.com

Index